Praise

"Anytime you enter the eye of the storm you need a guiding light, and with this book Dana gives us an inspiring and innovative path forward."

Billie Jean King, social justice and sports icon

"I have tried to bust myths for a long time, and I have had the privilege of psychoanalytic therapy to really uncover the unconscious imprints that drive all of us. There are external things that can help though, and this book is one. It's about motivation, not self-flagellation. Dr. Dana's guidance and suggestions are laid out in a way that all will understand and can apply. A very important tool!"

Jamie Lee Curtis, Academy Award–winning actor and *New York Times* bestselling author

"With *Dialed In*, Dr. Dana takes the guesswork out of the best practices required for continued individual delivery of high performance. She articulates a simplified, specific, and functional framework with applications for all aspects of life. This is a great read and an excellent resource!"

Andrew Jay Feustel, Ph.D., NASA astronaut (ret.)

"When I needed to be calm, clear, and focused, Dr. Dana Sinclair was a difference-maker."

Don Mattingly, baseball legend

"Winning, in any sector, means you need to show up when it matters most. Dr. Dana's work with the Dodgers helped us do that, and her new book will assist everyone to get to their best."

Mark Walter, controlling owner, LA Dodgers; Chelsea FC general partner

"Talent gets you in the game, but a distracted mind kicks you out. *Dialed In* dispenses with the typical platitudes and reveals the specific behaviors that separate great performers from the rest."

Daniel H. Pink, #1 *New York Times* bestselling author of *The Power of Regret and Drive*

"Dr. Sinclair is one of the world's greatest people, first and foremost. That makes her talent and knowledge for helping athletes get the best out of themselves more extraordinary. She is down to earth, she is relatable, and she will always be one of my favorite people! Thank you for being great, Doc!"

Kyle Lowry, NBA champion point guard

"Dr. Dana Sinclair has a passion for teaching and helping people become the best versions of themselves: quality colleagues or teammates who assume responsibility for their own performance."

Scott McCain, chairman of McCain Foods

"Dr. Dana Sinclair put everyone at ease and worked with the team to get us to the next level. Her approach is excellent!"

Nick Nurse, NBA champion head coach

"She saved my life. If it wasn't for Dr. Dana Sinclair, I would have lost my mind in some of the situations I faced. When she was our team psychologist in Anaheim, her calm and direct approach really helped stabilize and smooth out some of our performance issues."

Bruce Boudreau, Jack Adams Award–winning NHL coach

"In motorsports, we are always looking for an edge on the competition. Working with Dr. Dana opened my eyes to the difference that proper mental preparation makes. Her relatable approach made a noticeable difference in both driver and team performance in the pit stop environment of every race."

Scott Harner, team manager, Andretti Autosport

"Dr. Dana Sinclair and I have crossed paths numerous times over the years, usually in NHL rinks across North America. Her book gave me a real insight into exactly how she helps people—from professional athletes to business executives and everyone in between—perform at their best. And each chapter provides tools and strategies we can all use in our everyday lives to be the best versions of ourselves. I guarantee you will learn something!"

Christine Simpson, NHL broadcaster and Sportsnet reporter

"Dr. Dana Sinclair has deep insight on mental performance and the ways character matters even more than talent. She has been invaluable to me personally and in our Baseball Operations Department."

De Jon Watson, director of player development for the Washington Nationals

"I've had the great fortune of knowing Dana for many years. On top of her professional acumen and expertise in her field and at her craft, she is a phenomenal human being. Her approach is kind, positive, and affective. With years of experience and impact, she's an asset to whomever she touches. This book is reflective of all these things."

Stacey Dales, NFL Network national correspondent

"It can be challenging to find a resource that successfully weaves great depth of experience with pragmatic, real-world application, but Dr. Sinclair nails it. Her experience in the worlds of business, sports, entertainment, and entrepreneurship is as valuable as her relatability and common sense. This is a not-to-be-missed, can't fail resource for anyone serious about achieving and enjoying success."

Megan Buckley, chief operating officer, Hy's of Canada Restaurant Group

"As a longtime general manager of the Los Angeles Dodgers, I needed difference-makers to set us apart from the competition: we needed to turn the average player to good, good to great, and great to iconic. As you will read in *Dialed In*, that is Dana Sinclair's specialty. You will learn the methods necessary to become a difference-maker, to be at your best consistently, and to exceed in a mindful way."

Ned Colletti, former MLB executive

"Dr. Dana Sinclair worked with us as individual players, which really helped us get the most out of ourselves and contribute our best to the team."

Hampus Lindholm, NHL defenseman

DIALED
IN

DO YOUR BEST
WHEN IT MATTERS MOST

DR. DANA SINCLAIR

PUBLISHED BY SIMON & SCHUSTER
New York   London   Toronto   Sydney   New Delhi

SIMON &
SCHUSTER
CANADA

Simon & Schuster Canada
A Division of Simon & Schuster, Inc.
166 King Street East, Suite 300
Toronto, Ontario M5A 1J3

This Simon & Schuster Canada edition January 2024

SIMON & SCHUSTER CANADA and colophon are trademarks of Simon & Schuster, Inc.

Simon & Schuster: Celebrating 100 Years of Publishing in 2024

For information about special discounts for bulk purchases, please contact Simon & Schuster Special Sales at 1-800-268-3216 or CustomerService@simonandschuster.ca.

Interior design by Wendy Blum

Printed and bound in India by Replika Press Pvt. Ltd.

10 9 8 7 6 5 4 3 2 1

Library and Archives Canada Cataloguing in Publication
Title: Dialed in : do your best when it matters most / Dana Sinclair.
Names: Sinclair, Dana, author.
Description: Simon & Schuster Canada edition. | Includes index.
Identifiers: Canadiana (print) 20230182011 | Canadiana (ebook) 20230196128 |
    ISBN 9781982181871 (hardcover) | ISBN 9781982181888 (EPUB)
Subjects: LCSH: Achievement motivation—Popular works. | LCSH: Stress
    management—Popular works.
Classification: LCC BF503 .S56 2023 | DDC 153.8—dc23

ISBN 978-1-9821-8187-1
ISBN 978-1-9821-8188-8 (ebook)

To James Sleeth, you have always been my very best friend and are still absolutely stellar. I love my life with you.

And to our very lovely daughters, Hunter Sinclair Sleeth and Morgan Sinclair Sleeth, stay your forthright, funny, and sassy selves.

CONTENTS

Foreword

A little over thirteen years ago, I did what I always do when traveling alone: go to the gate, sit down, and find a best friend. I find someone whose presence calms me. We chat, talk about their favorite ice cream, whatever. I do this so that when I am feeling anxious or scared, or if it's a bumpy flight, I can look at my new best friend and if they look calm, I am calm. This soothes me tremendously, although I am sure there have been a few people thinking, "Who is this strange lady looking at me?"

On this particular flight to Toronto, I saw this lovely woman in a cream trench coat with beautiful chestnut hair and a huge welcoming smile. I'd found my person for this flight. Little did I know my new best friend would also be my seatmate. Her name was Dr. Dana Sinclair.

I am usually an anxious flier but on this flight I was also recovering from the birth of my third child and had a pretty bad case of postpartum depression. I was going back to work soon too, so I was very anxious.

Aside from her work in performance coaching, Dr. Dana also did reproductive mental health therapy. She had no idea that her flight home would become a five-hour therapy session. In the way that only she can, Dr. Dana immediately calmed me. She gave me tools to breathe and self-soothe—tools that would give my body and my mind a chance to heal.

Our flight (and session) came to an end, but it was the beginning of a trusted friendship I deeply value. And it was the beginning of countless sessions, from baby blues to my fear of driving on highways. Each time we speak, Dr. Dana knows what to say and how to *listen*. She knows how to talk to people to bring out their best. And while she doesn't disregard the mushy stuff, she teaches how to put that stuff in its place so it doesn't interfere with putting in the effort to be better the next time. Whether you're an actor like me, an athlete, a doctor, a race car driver, a hedge fund manager, or anything else, Dr. Dana will show you how to enhance your performance.

In this book, you'll first discover why some of the advice you've heard all your life is actually not helpful. How many times has a well-meaning teacher or parent said, "Just work harder!" as if that's all it takes? But don't worry, because Dr. Dana delivers real answers. You'll discover why staying calm, clear, and focused beats out natural talent in the long run, why you don't need confidence to succeed (though it's nice to have), how fear can manifest in surprising ways to derail performances, and why no one can give you motivation. And those are just some of the secrets to success you'll find here.

With all of that wisdom in mind, Dr. Dana then takes you through her three-step process for making your own performance plans, whether you're facing a daunting downhill slope or a tense boardroom. You'll learn the four key skills that you can practice as you read. And there are five revealing examples of different kinds of performers all going through the process with you. I find my new best friends in the airport terminal before a flight, but everyone you'll ever need is right here.

I have used Dr. Dana's tools in every audition, every role I take on. And I have used her tools to enhance my performance as a mother, too. That third baby I had just given birth to when I met my new BFF is now a high-achieving elite soccer player. So, guess who Dr. Dana's new client is? I know Dr. Dana will help her enhance her soccer performance, and she'll be all the better in other parts of her life, too.

I just adore Dr. D!

Alicia Coppola
Actor, writer, director, filmmaker
Los Angeles, 2023

Introduction

Step into My Office

We all want results. We all want to be good at what we do. But getting the most out of ourselves isn't always easy.

"I know you are a psychologist and work with a lot of athletes and businesspeople, but what do you *actually* do?" This is the question I am most often asked. A close second is, "Why would anyone want to talk to you, are they head cases?" I've learned that this usually means the person asking would like to chat about their own pressure moments.

My job is unique and specialized. It is under the radar for many and so I explain myself often. As a performance psychologist my role is to help people use their heads to be better at what they do. I talk about concepts and strategies that allow people to manage their emotions in the moment when they have to "go live" and want to execute well. I show people how they can learn to approach performance situations more calmly and with more clarity so they can get better results, even if they feel challenged or pressured by the task.

As a licensed psychologist specializing in performance, over the last twenty years I have worked with professional athletes and teams in the NFL, MLB, NBA, WNBA, NHL, MLS, IndyCar, WTA, PGA, and the Olympics. I also work with surgeons, students, executives, parents, coaches, and performance artists—actors, musicians, and more. I love working with anyone who wants to try to be better. Essentially, I help people focus so they can avoid errors, improve their skills, and get results. We keep it simple. We keep it fun. That's it.

Even these high-level performers can struggle under pressure. They get tense and nervous, they lose confidence, second-guess, and make mistakes. We are all capable of letting our mental approach undermine our abilities. But the good news? We are also capable of harnessing it to make it work for us in powerful ways.

Most of my time with clients is happily spent tackling performance issues and talking about practical solutions for getting results. Whoever they are and whatever they do, I hear the same concerns about performance. People want to talk about confidence, focus, fear, tension, and preparation. To become better, you need to know why you are great some days and not others. Do you know what you actually do right on those days when you feel as though you are performing effortlessly? Do you know what situations or thoughts undermine your ability to perform?

Research, experience, and common sense tell us there is a big mental component to performing well. You know you will perform better if you stay calm and focused, if you can minimize self-doubts and distractions. Learning to control your emotions under pressure—that is, when the moment is truly significant—will allow your talent and skill to show up and work for you.

In my practice, we focus on straight-up performance enhancement work—tools to help you right away. But general life events do pop up and are brought into the broader discussion. Relatively mild mental health concerns sometimes demand attention as symptoms associated with anxiety, depression, attention deficit disorder, phobias, and the like can interfere (often only in limited ways) with an individual's ability to cope and perform at their best. We then work to remove or at least mitigate these obstacles so that person can get back to their previous level of performance. Unfortunately, serious mental health conditions can also arise—

they do not discriminate and can affect anyone, anytime. But it's not why people come to see me and it's not the focus of this book.

In the world of mental health and emotional wellness, the areas of psychology, psychiatry, counseling, and psychotherapy can all seem to meld into a confusing bucket of similar proficiencies and zones of practice (though they are distinct). Although understanding is growing and attitudes are shifting in a big way, many people still hear the word *psychology* and immediately think illness and problems rather than satisfaction and results. My clients are looking for the latter and that is what this book is about.

Where does this work happen? I do meet people in my downtown office, but more often there is no calm room with comfortable seats and bright sunlight. Instead, it's the sidelines at games and during practices, in locker rooms, offices, hotel lobbies, planes, buses, gyms, at meals or dinner parties—anywhere. It's about finding a little time and space, even in chaos, to manage a distracted mind or tweak an already confident outlook.

How does it work? We talk, I listen (a lot). I assess and ask questions (also a lot) to find out how that person naturally thinks, feels, and behaves, not only in relaxed situations but in tough, distracting ones as well. Once we both understand how that person works—what is helpful and what hinders—it is so much easier to dial in on which behaviors and patterns need to be supported and which need to be suppressed.

My clients and I have talked about all aspects of performance, about how to think (and how *not* to think) when they want to perform at their best. They all come to understand that the core of performance is emotional control, being able to shift attention, in the moment, from distraction to action.

For instance, a neurosurgeon was curious if performance psychology could help him be better than he felt he currently was. There was nothing wrong with his work, but he wondered if there was anything about himself, his skills, or his style in the operating room that he could further refine.

I meet with high school and university students to show them how to stay calm and effective during an exam rather than waste precious time catastrophizing about "blowing it" before they have even started to work on it.

I have met with a financial advisor who was trying to deal with his highly critical, confrontational, and controlling boss. This is somewhat of a hot zone in my practice as I help people from all sorts of job areas try to navigate lousy bosses, difficult coaches, or overbearing parents.

What about setbacks, such as illness or injury? Health challenges can topple one's sense of identity, and prolonged recoveries can crush confidence. One of my young clients used some of the ideas and strategies found in this book to manage her tension and attitude through her (successful, thank goodness) chemotherapy treatments. An Olympic skier used the same strategies after a horrific crash that nearly killed him. He returned to the international race circuit with great success. Was he ever tough. He still is.

They can be seasoned professionals or aspiring teenagers, at the top of their game or struggling to feel good enough to belong, but they all want results. Often they are successful people and doing just fine in life, thank you very much, but are looking for a boost to take them to their best. They know their mental approach is key to inspired performance, and if they get more out of themselves in the challenging moments, they will feel more satisfied with their efforts. This satisfaction or sense of accomplishment means they have executed closer to their upper limits, which almost always means better results. And it feels wonderful.

Individuals, teams, and organizations are all part of my consulting practice, so I may be contacted by a specific person looking to meet or by someone on their behalf, such as coaches, presidents, managers, agents, parents, spouses, administrators, employers, or colleagues. I'm sometimes referred by health workers, too, such as physiotherapists, doctors, directors of sport science, trainers, etc. In addition to meeting clients in my office, I often travel for multiple teams in different leagues and consult with other organizations, some on a regular basis, others intermittently when needs arise.

For instance, the last time I signed with an NFL team, it was the head coach who requested performance psychology services for his players. He had a great approach and introduced me to the auditorium of players and staff during a morning meeting, allowing me time to talk to the group. This opening gave me a chance to quickly lay out my version of what I do and why it may be of interest to (hopefully) many of them. Typically, as with other teams, I would fly in every week or two during the season for a few days and meet with some individuals more formally in a boardroom, check in with others on the sidelines during practice or on game day, or end up going over game plans in the meal room sitting between the waffle maker and the kombucha machine—wherever it worked for the player.

Other organizations aren't so accommodating. Management may hire me and then point in the general direction of the locker room and say, "Go fix something or someone, and good luck." Once, I arrived for my every-two-weeks scheduled visit with an NHL team the day after the head coach was fired. The new coach was getting set up in his office and I went to meet him to ask what he had in mind for me for the next half of the season. His response? "Well, I don't know, I now have to go ask all the guys if they want a f-cking woman around."

While certainly meant to denigrate, I felt his bluster was more about him being tense in his new setting than an indication of who he really was as a person. I told him to please ask the players and let me know his decision before I had to leave in a few days to go visit another client. After that rough start it all worked out. Even though this guy didn't think anyone would want anything to do with "psychology," he came to see the strategies as simple, repeatable, and reliable. He even ended up using them himself. He found that trying to be better could only help, whether it was players working on their own performance needs or him preparing to be his best behind the bench. He even tried new ways to smooth his relationship with a prickly front office. In fact, working with this coach turned out to be one of my most enjoyable jobs in professional sport and we are still great friends.

I may do the occasional group presentation with a team's rookie class or present on a panel at a medical conference to give an overview of the process I use with clients, but the best work gets done one-on-one. In my experience, whatever your profession or the performance, nobody wants to listen too long to what other people do—they want to talk about themselves and learn what will work for them. People often need solutions in a hurry, and I am always struck by how much can be accomplished quickly, on the spot, even in stressful moments. This book is designed to bring these succinct, deliverable solutions to your pressure moments—when you need them most.

My approach with every client is to encourage an independent, self-determined performer, one who can learn to coach themselves to properly execute under pressure. To get past that limiting thought or annoying worry in the moment. No one needs to be dependent on a psychologist to coach them through their performances twenty-four-seven. You need to be able to deal with the unexpected, with any emotional overload, on your own. After all, you are the one who has to take that exam or deal with that critical boss.

Remember, your talent doesn't derail your performance; not *accessing* your talent in the moment diminishes your performance. Good performances, and even those that are just "fine," happen when your mental approach is clear, or at least not getting in your way. Whatever your talent level (even if you wish it were higher), you will be your best if you can manage your mind through some of the tougher stuff that pressure will throw at you.

We all want to gain satisfaction and confidence, but the ability to fight through mental noise when you feel unsure is surprisingly overlooked in conversations about leading a happier and more satisfying life. Being good at your job, being open and sensitive to your child's feelings, doing well in an interview, on a Zoom call, or on the golf course, even when you feel stressed or uncertain—all are straightforward and stellar opportunities to stay energized and on the positive side of your mental health.

Whatever you do, or want to do better, use the techniques and strategies in the following chapters to take action. Each chapter focuses on one concept that you can apply to life right away. You want to be able to get to your best so why not do this for yourself? What you need is right here.

I want to share with you the most relevant tools for performing at your best. From years of practiced and refined techniques, and actual client experiences as examples, you'll see how anyone can get the most out of their skills and efforts. I have changed names and obscured identities, but all my examples are real and true. I want to give insight into the emotional chemistry that people experience on good days and bad—because we all have those. And I want to simplify and demystify what it takes to be better no matter what you're doing. This book is for anybody and everybody because the practices that some of the world's highest performers use will work for you, too.

In part one you will find concepts and lessons about how to approach performing. Do you need to feel confident to do well? No, you don't. Can you really change the fact that you tend to freak out and fail under pressure? Yes, absolutely you can. Part two provides practices and strategies you can use to get actual results now, not a year from now, and will show you how to make and refine your own performance plans. And there's a section at the end of the book with review questions and quick tips to help you better understand your performance style.

Feel free to dip in and out of the chapters depending on what appeals to you in the moment—there is no single path to satisfaction and results. Think of this book as your own personal coach and guide, to be read in preparation of something that matters to you or referenced quickly on the sidelines as needed. Don't feel like you have to master all the strategies. First pick one, try it, and go from there.

I become wary when I see books on performance insisting that magical results and unshakable confidence for life are yours today if you just visualize that you are a powerful lion, or you'll be more focused and free from distraction if you chew gum (yes, I have really heard this advice given). It is important to be able to cut through the noise and slogans that saturate the "live your epic life" and "you can be whatever you want to be" self-help rhetoric. The truth is, I'm not interested in making you feel better—though I know you will when you see results. This book is about learning to get the best from yourself when it matters most.

Although this book talks about the experiences of others, I encourage you to think about your own performances for a moment. Are you unfailingly sharp under pressure? Are you routinely calm and focused on the task in front of you? Can you consistently rely on your skills whether you are driving a narrow fairway or presenting to your colleagues? If so, keep it up! But everyone can improve. If you are like most of us, and could be better and more composed, the real-life practical strategies in this book will help. They have been field-tested in high-pressure situations. Quite simply, they work.

This book is a safe space to reflect on your thoughts, fears, and behaviors regarding your good and bad performances in pressure situations. If you see yourself in the experiences of any of my clients, then those chapters may be particularly relevant to you. Regardless, I hope everything you find here leads you to be better than you were yesterday.

It takes courage to try to be good. Especially when the outcome of that performance is meaningful to you. A hockey player looking for more ice time and a student preparing for an exam have a lot in common. Becoming a more consistent performer—in a conference room, an operating room, or at an audition—is a life-changing skill. Whether you are an NFL quarterback dealing with a demanding and distracting teammate or a parent at a loss for how to help your teen relax before a big competition, it is important to know that you can coach yourself, and others, to be calmer and more focused.

You can be better. As one of my more spirited and colorful clients likes to say, "You gotta get the most out of what ya got! Right, Dana?"

Absolutely!

Part One

Myth Busting

Chapter One

Why Are Some People Better?

My first interview of the day is knocking at my door. I am back in Chicago for the yearly NBA Draft Combine and a well-dressed, smiling twenty-year-old ducks through the doorway and folds himself into one of the chairs at the conference table in this converted hotel room. He isn't smiling anymore because he realizes that I must be the dreaded psych lady. So I get to the point: "Yes, you are in the right place. This meeting is just going to be you and me, no scouts, no coaches, no management." I tell him up front that I am a performance psychologist and that I am going to do my best to get to know him, to find out how he is built from a psychological perspective. He relaxes his shoulders and his smile is almost back.

I ask him to first answer some questions on the computer that is set up in front of him. I sit with him for the fifteen minutes it will take to complete and then we chat about his responses, as I want to make sure I get my assessment right. I am also sure to tell him that there are no trick questions, which is true. We get started quickly as I only have this official time slot of thirty minutes to get a read on his performance style before the next prospect arrives at the door.

When it comes to performing under pressure, some people are just naturally better. Finding those with the potential to perform at a high level, consistently over time, is big business, especially in the sports and corporate worlds. Who is more likely to excel or disappoint? Who is the less risky choice? Who will fit into the current culture smoothly or require less supervision? Organizations are always looking to find and develop the best talent, but it's also important to understand how that talent will perform long-term. In other words, they wish to maximize their return on investment.

When selecting players, NBA teams will measure and test everything about that player from his vertical jump to his height (with shoes *and* without), and the length of his hands. Medical exams, game statistics, social media checks, and on-court drills and scrimmages are evaluated. Private investigators are even regularly hired to comb through player backgrounds to see what may be lurking. With so many disparate data points being considered (some useful, many not), it is not surprising that analytics has become increasingly routine in the attempt to identify those variables that best predict player potential or ability.

But what really separates one performer from the next? What insights determine who will be able to contribute more? "Talent" is the easy yet often incorrect answer. It's certainly an incomplete answer. Take Benny's NHL career, for instance.

He is so talented—what happened?

After six years in professional hockey, Benny was starting to feel a little less shiny and welcome. By now he was supposed to have amounted to more. He had thought he was doing fine and having a nice career, but the coaching staff, management, and even the media were starting to question his contribution to the team. Why wasn't he scoring more? Why was he late to practice? Why wouldn't he stop taking dumb penalties during the playoffs?

As a high draft pick, Benny should have been more productive on the ice. His scouting reports had all reflected how smooth his skating was and how skilled his hands were around the net. The reports also boasted, and this is real, that "he had a big ass," which apparently meant he would be tough to push off the puck. (I still think this notation should be filed under "fun facts" rather than objective selection data.) When the scouts and management interviewed Benny, they felt he was easygoing and talkative. He seemed eager to please (it was an interview, after all), so they assumed he was confident and coachable. They predicted that Benny would be a very valuable asset, they couldn't miss.

What happened? Why wasn't he as good as his skills indicated? Did they get it wrong? No, they didn't. He was definitely skilled. But in their excitement over his wrist shot, management ignored his personality characteristics. Benny's pre-draft performance-style report highlighted the potential problems to come. He was impatient, prone to frustration and snap decisions on the ice. He was a hothead. He was likely to take unnecessary penalties, often at crucial times in big games, because he was tense under pressure and undisciplined in the moment. His lack of seriousness meant that he glossed over his coaches' repeated requests that he stick to his assignments and not just do his own thing.

The head coach no longer trusted him on the ice. Management was done with him. They didn't want to invest more time and effort in trying to develop him as they felt they had already squeezed as much out of him as they could. They were disappointed and felt Benny had let them down. So they traded him. Benny's talent level hadn't changed (in fact, he had become a better player), but neither had his performance style. He had a hard time thinking through his actions and restraining himself under pressure. The organization had made the shortsighted mistake of assuming that top talent trumps all.

Assessing talent is one thing, but predicting success is entirely different. Benny's story illustrates one side of this coin, Cole's the other.

He turned out to be so good—what happened?

Cole was selected way down the list in the same draft as Benny. The scouting notes on Cole were unremarkable. Unlike Benny, he was not projected to be anything near a franchise player. But this team was progressive and decided to go one step further in their selection process. In addition to the report from me, I had been working on a performance-style tool that the scouts could use to rate their prospects on various observable behavioral characteristics, such as competitiveness, decision accuracy, and quality of effort. Cole wasn't especially talented, but he ended up at the top of their psychological attributes list. They didn't think he had the physical talent to amount to much, but based on his self-discipline and drive they decided to select him using one of their last picks.

Cole's mental- and performance-style highlights were impressive. He was patient, listened to coaching instructions, and didn't panic on the ice. He was serious about training and took time to analyze his play so he could make adjustments. His discipline meant he showed up on time, maximized his strength and conditioning, and worked on his weaknesses. His consistent approach allowed him to get the most out of his potential. Cole surprised everybody, including the team that drafted him. He became a superstar. The staff may have underestimated his hockey ability, but they had certainly nailed his ability to cope with adversity, demand the best of himself and his teammates, and stay focused over a season. In short, everybody missed his potential because talent doesn't tell the whole story.

If that's the case, that talent isn't everything, then what should we focus on?

Tap into your performance style

Simply put, your performance style is you being you. How you naturally behave, both on the job and more generally in life, provides powerful insight into how you will perform under pressure. If you don't understand your most prominent behaviors, you may miss what makes you good or how best to meet whatever challenges are waiting for you. Know which behaviors elevate your performance or rob you of results. Then modify your approach (or completely change it) to get more from any situation.

This book is about how to do that, but our starting point is understanding our natural reactions.

Think about your own performance style. Are you able to quickly move past mistakes or does biting self-criticism keep you on your heels and underperforming? How do you react to accurate but negative feedback? Do you keep your cool when you need to? When faced with uncertainty do you forge ahead with decisiveness or hang back and wait to see how things unfold before you try? If you understand which of your natural reactions can trip you up, you can learn to manage them more effectively.

For instance, if you know that you usually become passive and avoidant when presenting your ideas, you can learn to be more forceful and even stand your ground when challenged. If you are an overly quiet, reserved person, you can develop ways to express yourself and engage more effectively. Maybe you want to make a tight deadline without dissolving into a moody mess with those around you. Or sidestep your fear of failure and really try this time to crush your personal best in the upcoming 5k race, just like you do in training. Whatever your performance ambition, look a little deeper so you can enjoy connecting to your natural competencies and, more importantly, pinpoint those behaviors or tendencies that need to be refined.

What kind of performer are you? If you're naturally assertive you don't mind making decisions and putting them into action. You tend to take responsibility for your choices and are comfortable being accountable for them too. You deal with conflict in a straightforward manner and confront difficult situations with resolution in mind. You can delegate tasks with positive energy. You take initiative and are up for any reasonable challenge. You will be direct but respectful when you tell your boss she is being too heavy-handed with you or that you would like more responsibility. In general, you will take charge and get things done.

As with all styles and general tendencies, watch for a downside. If this assertive type sounds like you, when stressed you may feel as though you are losing or giving up some power. Watch that you don't become too demanding or argumentative and fight back when you don't need to. Listen longer before jumping into a debate and try making suggestions rather than telling someone what to do. Let the other person offer their opinion and make sure you aren't talking down to anyone. Compromising or agreeing to disagree can help you avoid an unnecessary argument.

What if you are more passive in nature? Modest and humble, steady and helpful, you are more comfortable and productive in lower-pressure environments. You will take a few calculated chances here and there but will approach risk with caution. You prefer others to speak up for you and you don't see the need for conflict or confrontation. Trustful, you thrive in a harmonious environment.

But sometimes disagreements are unavoidable. Be ready, when necessary, to address an issue or oppose a person. It's important to learn to not give in, and to resist being self-effacing (shrinking away may leave you feeling frustrated). Stay cool. Practice *saying* what you think rather than meekly mentioning your thoughts hoping someone will pay attention. Think about how you would like to present yourself and rehearse it in your mind—see yourself responding as you would prefer.

Does your mind move fast? If your thoughts are always moving quickly from one thing to another, you may be spontaneous and intense. If so, you like variety and are a master at managing multiple tasks. Anxious for results, you aim to get twenty things done every day (and when you don't, you are annoyed). You are fast-paced and restless. Energetic, you have a good sense of urgency and love being in the action. You are great at adapting to changing priorities. Impatient with the status quo, you may get bored easily, especially if you aren't that interested in the task.

The downside here is you may have a quick fuse and get frustrated easily, even if you usually recover quickly. Try not to decide things too fast; a touch more persistence and patience could have gotten a better result. Know that you tend to lose your focus under pressure and have a plan to manage it.

Perhaps you are more steady in your mood, tolerant and cooperative.

Your patience and consistency allow you to listen well and be a source of help and calm to others. You are naturally calmer, composed. You like to sit and focus for longer periods of time. Repetition and predictability are a comfort, so performing under unexpected change or shifting expectations can be exasperating. If your job requires fast output, or your teammates are scattered and impulsive, work may get stressful.

You react better to routine and planning, so be ready to adjust when your boss runs in demanding that everyone drop what they're doing and brainstorm solutions to a problem, now. Be ready to speed up your actions. Make timelines for yourself. Too much patience may result in missed opportunities, so you'll have to practice embracing the unknown.

Maybe your style stems from your sociability and persuasiveness. You are outgoing with your close friends and seek out new people. You love to be liked and resent feeling left out or ignored. Your trusting nature makes small talk easy, and people tend to find you charming. You like to look good and have your talents visible and recognized.

These are natural gifts for a performer, but the trick is to make sure you try to be objective in your interactions. Don't overtalk, you may miss out on something important. Be aware of the need to temper your optimism with a measure of seriousness so you can remain realistic. At times you may need to stop goofing around and refocus on your task.

What if you're the opposite: a serious person who likes to work solo or one-on-one? You are reserved, maybe shy and reflective. Skeptical too. You love your alone time and need it to function at top form. You are good with facts and like to problem-solve, to analyze and think, think, and think again.

Remember that talking more will help you communicate better. If you aren't sure of the plan, ask questions. When you do so, open your body language, don't be afraid to look people in the eye and speak with more inflection. Smiling never hurts, either. It's proven to lower your tension, and put others at greater ease, which can only help your performances.

Maybe you are a lover of certainty and rules. You work best when you have structure and know exactly what is expected. You are precise and self-critical. Perhaps you don't like to try something unless there is a high probability you will be able to hit your high standards (which also extend to those around you). You will over-worry about small (and big) things, and fuss when criticized, usually because you want to be excellent, or certainly not bad.

Watch for being sensitive and defensive when challenged as the person may be trying to help you improve. Avoid being overly critical of others and trying to be *right* all the time. Remember that things don't have to be done the way they have always been done. Keep the big picture in mind by staying open to new ideas. Check in with those who can help as you will feel relief and reassurance if you can confer your ideas or have your work checked.

Less common are the truly independent types. Self-reliant, you don't need precise direction and the security that comes with it. You are more likely to get the gist of something and then give it a go to see what happens and adjust from there. You love to express your opinion and are tenacious. People never suggest that you are a perfectionist. In fact, too many details stress you.

You may dismiss rules or directives that don't make sense to you and create your own work-arounds. As a big-picture type, you get yourself into trouble at times as you forget about the details and miss following up on small "unimportant" tasks (others will see this as unprepared and annoying). For these people, being on time and organized, prepared to address details that others value, will go a long way to improving performance.

These are the most common performance types I see. You may identify strongly with one or see yourself partly in several, but you should now have a better understanding of your own style and of those behaviors that may hinder your talent. Why are some people better? Because they modify their natural reactions in the moment. They use their heads. Any type of performer can excel, and this book will show you how.

To be clear, some performance styles are more desirable and easier to live with, for both you and those around you. But not everybody gets one of those. We all know that person who seems to float by adversity with ease and poise and get results. Good for them, I want them to enjoy the ride. But the rest of us must work to keep our tendencies in check. That can be hard unless you know the shortcuts. I call them the difference makers.

Chapter Two

The Difference Makers

Passive or forceful, quiet or gregarious, jumpy and tense or calm and tolerant, no one performance style guarantees success or ensures failure. But some characteristics definitely move you from great to greater, so why not act them out more often?

I am not suggesting you change your personality—you can't. I am encouraging you to change it up, for that specific event, situation, or interaction where you want to excel. Then you can go back to being the wonderful, natural you. It's not faking it—this is what the best do when they need to pull themselves together to be *their* best.

Take action

If you are a cautious, helpful, undemanding, or modest person, one that likes to "play it safe" and study a situation before you act, this difference maker is for you. You would be surprised by how many top performers are also mild and moderate by nature. But they have learned to make things happen rather than watch things happen. They initiate and *do*; they don't shrink from difficult situations. They don't take action all the time, mind you, but they know what they need to do to get things done.

Think of your natural assertiveness level on a scale. If you are generally a 3 (more passive and tentative), you don't need to become a 10 to take action and do a job well. That would make you more of the belligerent and overbearing type, and nobody needs that. Bumping yourself up to a 5 or 6 is all you need to get yourself to action and results.

Richie did it this way. I had only been working with this Major League Baseball team for a couple of weeks. I walked into the team training room, where players were getting treatment and preparing for the evening game, and I heard a player yell across the room, "Dana! My mind is all f-cked up!" I started to laugh but when I realized that he was serious, I told him, "Okay, so let's unf-ck it." I had no idea if Richie was feeling unprepared to be the starting pitcher that night or if something was going on in his life off the field. Either way, game time was looming and he wasn't happy.

We had only about fifteen minutes to talk so we went into speed-meeting mode. We sat in the dugout and I asked Richie what he thought was going on. He said he wasn't exactly sure but was definitely stressed about starting the game that night. I asked him some details about his previous few games and he replied, "My last two starts were my worst all season, so now when I am on the mound I just can't focus, everything is a blur." He wasn't thinking of throwing strikes, he was seeing himself throw wild pitches and being pulled from the game early.

He had to be able to take action out there on the mound in a couple of hours. So we decided that for this game he just needed to focus on "throwing properly" to get away from the worries of blowing it. He realized that he always maintained good command of the ball when he "stayed back" on the mound (not rushing forward) and when he "finished out front," meaning he fully extended his release straight to his target, right through the catcher's glove.

In this one brief talk together, he traded hesitation for decisiveness and pushed himself up the action scale by connecting to what he had to *do* more of. Richie finished his planned five innings with a win on his record.

Taking action didn't change Richie's personality; it helped him overcome a natural characteristic to make him perform better in the moment.

Slow down

Emotional control rules your ability to get results under pressure. The foundation of emotional control is a calmer, clearer mind. Owning the ability to self-soothe, to be able to calm down quickly, and to act with patience lowers your tension and puts you more in control. If you can slow down, you can mitigate a bad mood and settle your feelings of stress and worry. Quieting your thoughts means you'll argue less, hold back snap decisions, tamp down a rising temper, and stay focused on the task in front of you for longer. Slowing down actually gets you where you want to be faster and better.

Terry had been a federally appointed judge for three years. He was fast-paced, energetic, and liked to get things done. He was confident in how he handled his courtroom, his preparation was meticulous, and he managed difficult interactions smoothly and empathetically—all except for one. His natural energy and openness would often dissipate quickly when lawyers seemed unprepared. Late arrivals, shuffling of papers, missing files, and delayed responses all made Terry immediately angry. That anger wasn't the end of the world but it would negatively affect his behavior and he didn't like it. In this situation, Terry tensed up; he leaned forward in his chair, his eyes narrowed, and his jaw tightened. His tone became stern and dismissive. He would admonish his targets when they faltered. At these moments he felt reactive and less objective. It was the only time he became frustrated and distracted.

After we had dissected this one big derailer we talked about a solution he could employ quickly. He first had to change his physical demeanor. He told himself to sit back, sit tall, drop his shoulders, and loosen his jaw. Focusing on adjusting his body for a few seconds allowed him to circumvent his default attack mode. Then he made a point to remind himself not to take the sloppy behavior personally, that the lawyers were just inexperienced or unorganized (or both), not purposefully disrespectful of him or his courtroom. Then he could choose to discipline appropriately, if he thought it was warranted, or ignore the situation and move on. Either way, he reminded himself to keep his tone even and stay on task to avoid an emotional detour that diminished his performance.

Listen longer

As in talk less, or just be quiet more. Even a five-second delay in responding to someone can make the difference between conveying disinterest or confidence. Connecting to what the other person is saying for a little longer gives you the space to interpret their words as they intended, to minimize wrong-headed assumptions, or absorb information and emotion that make for more objective decisions.

Those who aren't natural listeners tend to be too busy talking at people or chatting about themselves. They interrupt. They wait for a break in the conversation so they can jump back in and resume what they were just saying. They get distracted by focusing on their next response or they may mentally drift off to unrelated thoughts. If you don't bother to hear what people are saying, you may not clearly see a helpful (or harmful) perspective or catch details that matter. When it comes to great listening, most people will stop short rather than go too far.

As the head coach of a successful NHL team, Matt was serious about being the boss. During games he yelled and swore and shouted, just as his coaches had done when he was a pro player. He constantly questioned the officials and ignored feedback from his assistant coaches. He criticized his players on the ice but only those on the bench could really hear him. Eventually Matt's players caught on that as soon as they hit the ice for a shift, he would be picking them apart for everyone to hear.

Assistant coaches and team leaders soon went to Matt to discuss their frustrations and concerns, that his talk behind the bench was confusing and distracting. They pointed out that hassling the referees was resulting in unnecessary penalties against the team. Matt's responses were swift and unyielding. He was in charge and all they had to do was stop whining and listen to him. He was focused on what he had to say and completely missed that the team found him to be combative and overly critical.

Players started to tune him out. Coaching staff stopped bringing innovative ideas to meetings—they never got used anyway. He was facing a mini mutiny, all because he wasn't listening. Finally, Matt was ready to adjust.

We worked out a plan, a few simple reminders written down that he actually took to the bench with him during the game. We decided together on the messaging: "Say less, stay cool, and shut up." He also made a deal with his coaches, agreeing to listen to them when they told him to tone it down with the players or back off the referees—they had to be firm, but it worked! He began asking his coaches for more feedback so they were at least part of the discussion rather than always feeling talked at. When speaking with players he would ask questions as to why they made that switch on defense or made a particular pass. When the player was responding, rather than cutting him off, Matt would remind himself to "Wait, let him talk, take in what he is trying to tell me." He may still ream out the player but at least his reaction would be based on good data. The players felt the difference. Matt wasn't perfect, but by working to listen longer he was adding to the team's energy rather than depleting it.

Drop the details

Detail-oriented people strive to be precise. They like the guidance provided by rules and systems and do well with order and structure. Tolerating uncertainty can be uncomfortable so they look for high odds of success before trying something, especially if it's unfamiliar. Self-conscious and self-critical, they like to know what is expected of them and want to get it right the first time, every time. Perfectionists like this are excellent at completing assigned tasks and have an eye for anticipating what could go wrong.

However, precise people can get caught up in the very details they love so much. The standards and expectations they set for themselves and others can be unrealistically high and they may be seen by others as fussy or hard to please. Being overly critical of details that don't contribute to the big picture, or don't really matter, can push people to distraction. Or worse, an overzealous enforcement of too many rules or opinions can promote frustration and even antagonism. Knowing when to relax your grip on details will not only advance a project but your performance as well.

Britt was killing it as a structural engineer at a prestigious firm. She had been on the job for four years and her performance reviews were awesome. She was polished and respectful when dealing with others. She was meticulous and very attentive to accuracy. She felt if it wasn't perfect, it wasn't good enough. She analyzed situations carefully and avoided disharmony. She would seek the approval of her boss before moving ahead to the next phase of a project. She was so good at her job that she was promoted to manage an important project. She was elated and looking forward to continuing her individual success.

It didn't take long for Britt to start feeling anxious and unsure. She had always completed her work on time but now found herself falling behind despite working longer and longer hours. She had always been able to rely on her superiors to make the final decisions but now she was the decision-maker. When she had tight deadlines, she began to worry more about making mistakes. She kept checking and rechecking her work. She didn't let others on her team complete some of their assigned tasks as she felt it would be easier and faster to just do them herself. She would pounce on the small errors of others without mentioning that the broader work was outstanding. Her team wasn't learning or gaining the valuable experience they were looking for; they were discouraged and felt that Britt didn't have confidence in them. Rather than delegate and oversee, she controlled and procrastinated. She was drowning in details and had lost sight of the big picture.

Britt needed to start dropping the details and move on. After some discussion (and some excuse making), she decided on two ways to advance her performance and her project. First, to get the best results, she realized she needed to share the work, even the tasks she had always loved to do. She would resist trying to control each aspect of the project, especially the smaller, less critical items. She knew her team was competent, so she began to hand off assignments to her people and spend more time discussing their ideas and progress rather than doing the work herself.

Second, Britt also needed to make decisions faster. She was reluctant to hand her work up to the next level until she felt it couldn't be criticized, and so wasn't moving the project forward in a timely manner. How did she adjust and get her project moving? She limited her "fuss time" by reducing the checks and rechecks. Britt actually set a limit on the time spent and the number of checks she was comfortable with and made an effort to stop when she reached her cutoff number. Otherwise, she would just keep searching for more supporting data rather than making a decision with the best information available. She also began asking a trusted colleague to do a quick review of the tricky sections. This external check allowed her to mitigate much of the discomfort she experienced when she had to make important decisions.

Britt found practical ways to drop the details and better manage the overall project. Deadlines create pressure, which push a perfectionist like Britt to cling to what is more easily controlled. But she found that staying on top of her tendencies gave her a newfound relief and energy, which her team felt too!

Check yourself

Whether you're the type of person who always thinks you aced it or breathes a huge sigh of relief when your performance is over, look back on it to see what you can learn. It is hard to improve if you don't know how or what you have done. Checking yourself may take courage but it is the smart way to get ahead.

Blake and I have a long history. She walked into my office years ago as a young woman referred by a psychiatrist for some practical help with anxiety and panic. We spent time talking through her concerns and deciding on useful strategies to stabilize her emotions when she felt vulnerable to stress. Occasionally we would pop out of the office and put her strategies into action. We would ride the bus or order coffee in a crowded shop, things that helped her regain her independence. We started each meeting by reviewing how well she had used her strategies the previous week, highlighting what went well and what didn't. This check would set the tone for our work. Once Blake was able to consistently settle her most debilitating symptoms, we said our warm goodbyes and she moved on with her life.

Five years later, I heard from Blake again. She had cancer and felt a psychological refresher would help her deal with the anxiety and discomfort of her upcoming treatments. We revisited her performance style to anticipate ways she may feel vulnerable in this setting. I joined her for her first treatment to talk through strategies that would give her some tranquility and relief.

After each treatment she checked herself. She would rate how well she thought she handled her anxious feelings. She would note what kept her composed and when her tension rose. Then she would adjust her preparation with purposeful breathing and imagery practice (literally imagining different scenarios, see chapter 15) between and during treatments. She would listen to music or bring a friend to sit and chat with. She was increasingly encouraged by the tangible improvements in her emotional strength and bodily calm. We were both thrilled and relieved when she got the all clear from her doctor and was free to once again move on with her life.

Many years later, Blake and I were back working together. She had recently relocated across the country and loved her new home, but she was facing a new pressure. She needed a job and kept missing out. Each interview was a struggle. She felt she was slipping back into being too emotionally reactive when stressed and it was affecting her ability to connect with people. She finished her note saying: "I have to deal with my performance and I think getting some psychological help is the healthy thing to do."

I was impressed. Blake knew she needed to change her approach to move forward. And she had the courage to try. When we spoke she was firm: "I need a job but I hate interviews. I never interview well—it is one of my worst skills. I feel like I sabotage every single one and now I am reticent to try as I assume it won't go well." I went back to the structure she previously found helpful. "You used to do a good job of checking yourself, what have you found when you do that now?"

She'd completely forgotten! She explained she prefers to fully distance herself from any thoughts about the interview as soon as it's over because it was just too uncomfortable and disheartening.

We put together a plan for her upcoming Zoom interview to help her stay connected to her behavior and the questions being asked. She had a short list next to her computer she could refer to when she needed it. She had written, "Stay calm and breathe, sit up, *listen* to the question, less is more (meaning less talking), *slow down*, try to smile." She knew doing any of these would be helpful.

And she knew she had to check herself when she didn't get yet another job. She rated herself a 4 out of 10 in terms of her performance and felt that she needed a 7 or 8 to be successful. But she was doing some things well now: "I researched the job thoroughly. In the beginning of the interview, I was winning points." She then listed what did not go so well: "But then I got more tense, lost focus, and started to ramble. I was analyzing myself while I was answering the questions. I went blank on easy answers and ended up freezing. I panicked when I realized that the panel was losing patience with me, so I gave up. By the end I was unresponsive. I realized I really wanted that job and didn't stick to the plan at all. I need to chill out and just try to be myself."

It was a process of constant self-evaluation and improving her plan. But eventually she got the job she wanted. By that time, she self-rated at a 7 and felt good about it. She still approached the interview as an inquisition but was able to shift her attention to the questions being asked. Job well done.

A few months later I called Blake to, well, check in. She reflected on her mental health and approach over the years succinctly: "Back then I was an intensely anxious person prone to panic. Whenever that demon tries to surface now, I kick it to the curb. Things have definitely changed. I have my strategies but now I make sure to check myself rather than run from any negativity or discomfort. I realize that it has always helped me cultivate peace in my life."

I have noticed that many top performers naturally use some, if not all, of these difference makers at different times. They also apply these skills to more than one type of performance. And for those of us who don't naturally do it, now that you recognize these ideas, you can use them too.

Chapter Three

The F Word

That's right, fear. Fear shows up in many ways. Fear of what? Of not being good enough or of disappointing yourself or others. Of not feeling confident or in control, of feeling vulnerable or being rejected. Of embarrassment, of not being perfect, or of making a mistake. Of expectations, or of what could go wrong even though it hasn't yet, but it might!

Fear of failure is powerful and prevalent. It is an unavoidable part of a striving life. I am not referring to the extreme perfectionism that can lead to irrational and persistent fear, or to the harrowing anxiety that defines phobic reactions (a colleague once told me about a client who had a phobia of muffin tops, the baked version not the excess roll over your pants version). I am talking about the ordinary, simple worries and thoughts that can lead to inaction, to holding back, to giving up before or during a task, or to temper tantrums—all of which can only undermine how you perform.

Instinctively, we want to protect ourselves from disappointment, frustration, and shame. Uncertainty, as in not knowing how things will turn out or what your results will be, tends to fuel overthinking and self-criticism. It is very difficult to perform well when your mind is focused on what could go wrong rather than on what you need to do to make it go right. You may use excuses to insulate yourself from the emotional discomfort that can come with performing below your expectations or desires. You may feel like anything you do won't be good enough, so why even try to achieve a good result? Although some people are more sensitive to the emotional turmoil created by attempting something unfamiliar or meaningful, we all experience it.

Face those fears

Not long ago, with a day's notice, I flew to London to spend a week with a professional tennis player and his support team including agents, medical staff, and fitness trainers. He even had personal hitters at his disposal. Travis, his coach, is easy to work with. We could talk about what mental and technical adjustments may best help his player stay focused on court during a close set at a Grand Slam tournament. We have experienced the huge joy of watching his athlete compete exceedingly well in the toughest of circumstances. We have also endured the tensions of addressing the more delicate issues that can accompany high levels of success, such as an inflated sense of entitlement and, unfortunately, some bad behavior.

On this occasion, my mission was more off-court crisis management than on-court performance tweaking. Let's just say that the player had enjoyed his off-season with a little too much enthusiasm. It is amazing how novel opportunities, new people, and fun distractions can quietly derail an otherwise professional training regimen! In short, the player needed to check his motivations and get back to a more serious focus.

On day two of our training week, Travis interrupted our chitchat on the way to the practice court. With the player's agent listening intently, Travis said, "What do people talk to you about anyway? I just don't get it. I suppose I understand that people may have some personal worries or can be bothered or nervous at times especially during big tournaments with trying to play well on top of the demands of sponsors and media and all that, but why would anyone think they needed to talk to you? I mean, I wouldn't have anything to talk to you about or even know what to say if I had to talk to you about myself."

I thought he had finished but there was more. "Also, how do you get people to talk to you? Do they even want to talk to you? Do they just open up, or do you try to make them talk by asking them specific things?"

Wow. I had to take a moment to think. I had worked with this guy through some highs and lows, including some of his own (which he clearly did not recognize or remember), and all of a sudden he didn't seem to know what I was doing there?

Something wasn't right. But then I clued in. For the first time, things were not going smoothly for us as a team (due to the player's dedication to party time). Travis was stressed. He was worried that he would say the wrong thing to the player at the wrong time. He was having doubts that maybe he wasn't good enough as a coach to manage the player and the team. So, he did what many people do when they feel threatened—he became defensive.

If we were going to do our best for the player, I knew Travis and I needed to talk even if it was going to be uncomfortable. After all, being honest and facing your anxieties can be daunting for anyone. Over dinner, I stated the obvious: while his player was rising in the world rankings, so too were the expectations (from parents to sponsors) to keep improving and winning. I then bit the bullet and gently invited him to say what he was so tense about. We sat there for what I am sure was an entire minute before he said that he hadn't been in this big a spotlight before and was feeling pressure, mostly from himself, to make sure his athlete performed well at every tournament, no matter what ridiculous things were happening in the player's life off the court. As the leader of the team, he was afraid he wouldn't be able to guide his athlete through these tough moments and may even lose his job as a result.

Balking at undesirable feelings, like inadequacy, may at first seem like a slick way to maintain outward composure and inward emotional control.

But over time, hiding from yourself will stifle your performance. If you are distracted by ruminations of failure or frustrations that seem constant or insurmountable, how can you be calm enough to focus clearly on what you need to do to perform well?

It turned out that simply having the courage to talk about and acknowledge the worries that were starting to feel overwhelming, and hearing that these fears were completely normal given the situation, were all Travis needed to regain his usual composure. Rather than feel flawed as a leader, he was able to lessen his anxiety about the near future enough to turn his attention away from the "what ifs" of the situation and get back to his usual sophisticated coaching and communication approach.

Fear will always come and go. Confronting your fears, rather than resisting or avoiding them, will lessen their hold on you and allow you to move forward. Voicing his fear was enough for Travis to move past this roadblock. But more often people need to think a little deeper before they can accept and deal with what frightens them.

Getting in your own way

How does fear actually interfere? It goes something like this: You want to be really good at something that is important to you and you know you have the ability to achieve it (or at least to be better). All you have to do is try to execute the task in question properly. Because if you do what you have been practicing, then you will do well.

For example, if you golf, you know your tee shots will likely go farther and straighter down the fairway if you remember to align the clubface with your target, focus on a low and slow takeaway, and hit through the ball at impact so you extend your swing fully. Completing even just one of these three actions, or performance cues, will enhance your swing and thus your shot. Technically, you will have executed correctly and will have given yourself a chance to better your score. Whether you are a duffer or a professional, you will be pleased because you have performed to your ability. Easy enough.

But wait. You may start to think, *What if I really try and it doesn't go well? What if I play well but it still isn't good enough and once again my ball ends up under a bush or in a bunker? That might mean I am not as good as I think I am, or want to be, or as talented as others say I am. That would be terrible.*

So how does someone protect themself from being disappointed? Self-sabotage of course. Excuses, as opposed to real reasons, may begin to surface. "That one bad hole early on the front nine really destroyed the rest of my game." Or, "That foursome in front of us was so slow I just couldn't stay focused." And the often used but still pitiful, "If only I had stayed hydrated and had a snack!" Whatever the excuse, it comes from the same fear: the problem can't be me, it must be something else.

You may not even be aware that you are doing this to yourself. This mental noise acts as a self-protective screen by which you can filter and soften the reasons for failure. Here, the goal is to verify for yourself and others that your sub-standard result is undeserved and not your fault. If the conditions had been right, or fair, you would have been better.

Self-sabotage keeps alive your hope that you can still do it! That you can still reach your personal best score or get that dream job or lose those annoying ten pounds, eventually, somehow.

If you want to be better, you need to change it up. In my office, it is usually quite clear when someone is getting in their own way. They relinquish personal agency and focus outside of themselves. I often hear, "I can't because . . . ," "Nobody ever helps me," or "They never give me enough time to prepare properly." If this sounds like you, take a moment and ask if you are the one holding yourself back. You will enjoy the relief of knowing you have finally recognized this self-imposed barrier. And better yet, you can now turn your attention to the task before you without all the distracting subterfuge.

Freak-outs

The fear of failure tends to show up when we think we are bumping up against our own limitations. So, what happens when you let fear push you a little too far? Super fears can show us.

Ryan, a young finance executive with whom I worked, struggled with public speaking, which of course is considered a super fear by many. He had just "botched" a big presentation to his superiors and said, "I knew the material, but I became so occupied with trying *not* to appear nervous that I rushed through my slide deck and made mistakes and then I just wanted it to be over with. I could even feel my face going red. I really hate that."

Ryan had experienced a classic performance freak-out, letting distractions hinder his talent and compromise his performance. He wanted to appear confident and knowledgeable, but he failed to prepare for the heightened emotional state he would be facing. He lost control of his breathing and thus his ability to stay calm and connected to the material he had prepared. He knew he could do better.

Taking an exam is another high-fear zone for many people. Whether you are taking a final math exam, a standardized test that will open the door to a university you covet, or examinations that will let you advance in your career, test taking can be intense and intimidating. Worries about results, the significance of a brilliant one or the consequences of a poor one, can disrupt your ability to be sharp in the moment, during the actual exam. Walking into a supervised exam space, being asked to turn in your devices, and sitting in silence with a big clock looming over the room can certainly be distracting. Your knowledge is clearly intact and waiting to be unleashed but your increased tension has the potential to cloud your problem-solving abilities. Simply put, you can know all the answers but if you freak out you will not be able to fully access your excellent preparation.

Sadie was overjoyed when she opened her provisional acceptance letter from the Ivy League university of her dreams. All she had to do now was keep up the good work through her final exams and she would be moving into her first dorm room. As her exams got closer, her expectations went into overdrive and she began to bombard herself with unhelpful and silly thoughts like, *Did I study the right stuff? What if I don't get financial aid? What if I run out of time?* Even *I hate big exams.* Or her go-to when she was really stressed: *What if I forget everything when the exam starts and they cancel my admission?* To avoid a classic performance freak-out, like what Ryan had experienced, we worked on a Freak-out Plan.

Since Sadie had already realized that her current mental approach would lead to unfocused, bad test taking, we didn't waste time talking about how fearful she felt. (We both knew!) Instead, we talked about what she usually *does* when she does well on an exam:

*   I arrive early, I pack my school bag the night before.
*   I read over the test in full.
*   I ask for clarification when unsure of the question.
*   I highlight key words in the question.
*   I start with the questions I know.
*   I ALWAYS go for partial marks.

So far so good! These actions have always helped her do well. But if the fear is big, plan a few more strategies to ensure that you can rein in those negative thoughts when they start to push you further into worries of failure and away from constructive action. Sadie added realistic and helpful self-talk:

*   Take the time to settle in, slow down, and start the exam correctly.
*   I can do this. I did get into that university, after all!
*   I've been doing fine all year, so chill.
*   I've done the practice questions, I've been studying, I've got this.

Talking yourself through an event is an exceptional way to stay calm and on task (chapter 14). Most of us live with an active inner voice in our heads, so why not harness that energy? If you don't you will end up overexpressing your fears. When managing your internal chatter, stick with truthful or even neutral comments, like Sadie did. Overly optimistic affirmations such as "I am fabulous and I am going to crush this thing!" may hold truth but are not enough to sustain you through your high-fear zone.

Sadie had one more strategy to add. She knew that to be clear-minded and connected to the exam questions she needed to be calmer and breathe properly (chapter 12). She decided that her number one focus, the one thing she should do if things felt out of control or she forgot everything else, was to just breathe. Simple but productive. Her final plan looked like this:

Before Exam

* Review my plan!
* Well, I have decided to take this thing so I may as well. calm down, shut up about it, and do the best I can!
* I've got this.
* Now breathe slow, exhale, and get my shoulders down out of my ears.

During Exam

* Keep breathing slow and loosen my shoulders.
* Keep focused on the QUESTION until the very end.
* Go for partial marks!

#1 Focus (Just in case I forget everything!)

* Breathe it out.

Now that Sadie's plan was in place, she could see a concrete way to quiet her exam fears. She knew that even if she didn't feel very confident or calm, she could still perform well by quickly shifting her thoughts and actions over to her plan. For people like Ryan and Sadie who experience unsettling reactions to certain pressures, a Freak-out Plan can be the only difference between a bad performance and a good one. We'll look at making plans like this in more detail in part two, but for now just remember that fear can be managed by preparation and simple cues in the moment.

The extreme

Some fears are totally justifiable. What about environments that are not only pressure packed but pose a real threat of possible illness, injury, or even death? First responders, including frontline healthcare workers, paramedics, law enforcement officers, military personnel, corrections staff, etc., all face the potential of violence and trauma in their daily work. Race-car driving, rock climbing, as well as contact and collision sports from hockey to football, all expose their participants to physical risk, especially in the professional arena where the strongest, fastest, most highly skilled people on the planet compete. Are these people immune to fear?

No, of course not. Take skiing for example. People love to say that downhill skiers are literally nuts or, at the very least, reckless to do what they do. My first job in Olympic sports was working on the Alpine Ski World Cup circuit with the Canadian men's speed team. We were in Kitzbühel, Austria, for the world-famous Hahnenkamm race, which is the Super Bowl of downhill racing. It is absolutely notorious, the most dangerous and difficult race in history—and so the most prestigious, too. The speeds reach up to 140 km/h, or about 87 mph (just think of driving on the highway). The demanding terrain is unmatched on the circuit. There are helicopters at the ready to airlift crash victims to the hospital. The technical skill and mental focus required to make it down fast, and in one piece, make it a thrilling event for spectators and athletes alike.

Even those who win the race talk about the fear! But that fear is mitigated by talent and the skills to negotiate the course. What is an extreme situation for some is accomplished almost casually by others. In other words, they aren't as scared as us. They still have to manage their fears but their fears center largely on results and expectations. They want to do well, like any performer. They work to calm their minds and stay clearly focused on skiing an efficient line from gate to gate so they can put pressure on each ski at the right time to powerfully carve a fast turn. The truth is, they know they have a job to do and are inspired to do it. Some are better than others, of course, but they are capable of getting to the finish. At some point thoughts about injury may float through their minds, but like any performer, they are trained and do their best to stay connected mentally to what they need to do in each section of the course in real time during the race. In short, they have the skills and abilities needed to navigate the exhilarating madness ahead of them. They are not about to do something stupid.

Unlike me. In preparation for race day, all the racers meticulously train on the course. Initially they "slip" the course to get a feel for the terrain and the turns. They hop into the course through the start gate and lightly sideslip the course, stopping and starting all the way down to inspect the line they will ski on race day. The coaches and some support staff do this as well. I didn't *need* to slip the course, but I wanted to because it would be fun (scary too, but I could go slow). And it always gave me an even greater appreciation of just how spectacular these athletes are.

On this particular day, it was time to head to the start to inspect the course. Up I went all excited, in part, to be able to say I made it down the celebrated course (even though I would be dawdling all the way down). I slid into the start gate, eased my ski tips forward onto the course, and found that they were hanging over air. I kept trying to scoot out far enough to at least see the ground in front of me, but it wasn't there. It was like I was teetering on the top of a mountain, which of course I was. There I lingered, but not for long. I quickly reassessed my ski skills and made the only prudent decision. I backed the entire way out of the start hut past all those racers and coaches waiting to get on the course. I then went directly to the lodge for a deliciously strong espresso. I was afraid of mangling myself, unlike the real skiers who were fearful of a poor result. Some were nervous, some were internally freaking out. But they all had to manage their emotions just like the rest of us.

The postscript to my sad little tale of fear on the mountain is that during my lovely coffee break I started to notice a bit of commotion around me. Something had happened on the course. I recall lots of groans and multi-language swearing. It turns out that my counterpart working for another country had bravely given it a go himself (even after witnessing my backout). Apparently, he didn't make it very far before becoming a human torpedo and taking out all the German television cables along the top section of the course. Even now, whenever we bump into each other, we can't help but have a good laugh about that day.

Everybody, at some point, has experienced the distraction of fear and its negative impact on performance. Some people tend to freak out at the slightest hint of pressure while others handle their concerns or fears with amazing equanimity.

Remember, I am not talking about performing in situations where you're not fully invested. I am focusing on those situations or events that are meaningful and thus likely to generate fear and pressure. For instance, you may feel relaxed and in charge when presenting your innovative ideas to your manager but may feel more nervous and diffident when you present those same ideas to your company president along with the board of directors.

Fear is relative. And it doesn't skip over a first responder, big-wave surfer, concert pianist, actor, or neurosurgeon. Fear will find you no matter your skill set or level. Expect it and accept it, as it is all about how you manage that fear in those moments that matter to you. Fear of failure will stop some people in their tracks so they won't even attempt to try something. Others will push onward with calmness and composure in the most stressful situations and achieve great results. Will mental turbulence stop them from performing? Not likely, but it can stop them from performing at the level to which they are capable. The trick is to learn how to recognize this tendency, call yourself on it, and move past it.

Making a plan to handle your fears, whether they are minor or supercharged, will be discussed more in part two. First, we need to look at how a lack of confidence isn't the big deal you think it is and understand that it isn't a cure for fear. And we'll see why others seem to have it when you don't.

Chapter Four

Confidence Is Overrated

Kristen had just won a golden ticket on *American Idol*. She was through to Hollywood Week for the next round of auditions and another chance to advance in the reality show singing competition. When she called, I expected to hear joy and jubilation in her voice, but she sounded frazzled. "I am not at all happy about my performance, I should have been better, I was way too nervous and afraid of messing up. The cameras, the judges, it was a really big deal and I was psyching myself out." Even though the judges told her she had "star quality" and wanted to work with her, Kristen kept talking about how good the other singers sounded, how she was in over her head, and that she would soon be cut from the show. She said, "I really, really want this, but I need to have that confidence that other people seem to have. I can't do it if I am not confident."

I managed to interrupt her long enough to mention that she had, in fact, just done *it* without feeling remotely confident or even comfortable. I added that she must know something about performing or she wouldn't have made it that far. Kristen was silent for a moment, then calmly said, "Well, I do have a really good voice."

When pressed to think a little more objectively, Kristen connected to the core fact that she could perform at this level. She needed to keep this evidence front and center mentally so she could more easily connect to her talent and spend less energy occupying herself with imaginary potential disasters. We decided to get to work on how she could better manage the outsized, negative reactions that seemed to bubble up when she felt the pressure of a big moment. In the coming weeks she would need to be able to find her voice on demand—and searching for confidence wasn't the answer.

What is confidence?

Confidence is a belief or a feeling that you can get something done. It is a measure of trust in your ability to perform well and get the desired results. *What a vague and intangible concept!* How often have you heard someone say, "Just trust yourself and be confident," or "All you need is some confidence"? Telling yourself to be confident doesn't make it so.

We pursue confidence because it makes us feel more comfortable and therefore more able. Life feels a little easier when you have it and a little more intense when you don't. And people love to talk about confidence, usually because they worry they don't have enough of it. I regularly hear comments like, "I won't be able to play my game until I get my confidence back," "I just know it won't go well today because I don't believe I can do it," "The others seem so mentally strong, I don't have a chance—where did all my confidence go?" It is astounding how easily we can let a *feeling* derail what we are capable of *doing*.

Confidence is variable and unreliable, as it can seemingly change from day to day, hour to hour, and, annoyingly, even minute to minute. Have you ever walked out of an exam feeling like you absolutely nailed every question, but by the time you got home were consumed by thoughts of certain failure? Confidence in our abilities or expectations can change surprisingly quickly and without notice. Even for the most self-assured people, confidence can be fleeting. That is why one must look beyond feelings of confidence when preparing to perform and during the performance itself.

You may be wondering: Don't I need confidence to succeed? No, you don't. Confidence is more of a preference than a need. You might want it, but you can perform well without it. People want to believe that elite performers possess an unshakable, unwavering confidence that is the basis of their success. But champions are definitely not always confident.

One of my clients described her first Olympics as an "emotional freak show." After qualifying for a freestyle final, she found herself at the start with only one more run between her and a medal. All she had to do was get down that mountain on her feet; it would take less than a minute. She knew a good result was possible, but there was a problem. She wasn't confident at all—in fact, she was falling apart emotionally and couldn't calm down. "I was negative all day, I even cried. I wanted to win but didn't think it would happen for me."

Despite pressure unlike anything she had ever felt, she managed to suppress her distractions in the moment by reminding herself to connect to the task in front of her and talk her way through her tougher tricks and jumps. To her surprise and relief, she coasted into the finish area as the Olympic champion. This gold medalist still says, "I'll never feel like I am good enough when I compete, but I know I will perform well if I just think more about what I should be doing on the course."

Many champions have similar stories about confidence. Another Olympic gold medalist said that his confidence was fragile and that he could feel doubt one moment and self-assurance the next, no matter the competition. Once he realized he would always have to work to find the emotional balance between distraction and focus, he accepted it as part and parcel of trying to achieve.

Effortless confidence is not essential to stand on top of the world. The ability to manage a wandering mind and stay connected to the immediate task is what works.

Confidence isn't the answer

Feeling confident is ideal, but it doesn't guarantee anything. You can feel exceedingly confident in your ability to win the race but suddenly hit the last hurdle and stumble across the finish in fifth place, wondering what happened. Feeling relaxed and unconcerned as you hop into your department Zoom meeting doesn't always protect you from a sudden surge of tension and hesitation when it is time for you to give your input.

Max was one of Major League Baseball's best pitchers. He always prepared well and was justifiably very confident in his game. The first time he took his team to the league championship series, he was stunned when his personal performance faltered and the team failed to advance to the World Series. He told himself that his unexpected poor showing was a fluke as his regular season play had been spectacular.

The following season he was again almost unbeatable and looked forward to dominating his starts in the playoffs. But the pattern repeated. For a second time he failed on the mound and the team lost their chance to appear in the World Series.

Afterward, we talked about what needed to happen differently next season. He twigged that because he always felt confident in his ability, he didn't anticipate or plan for any distractions or stress to disrupt his usual excellent mental control. As a result, he wasn't prepared to be his best. He had become so used to just stepping on the mound and throwing strikes that he didn't have an antidote at the ready for emotions that seemed to hijack him out of nowhere. His mind had excitedly raced ahead to the World Series when he wasn't yet there. He hadn't thought about his mental game since he was a nervous rookie, so he simply hadn't noticed that his focus was drifting.

Getting distracted by the potential of the World Series was enough to tighten him up and alter his arm extension just enough to affect his pitches so that more batters got a piece of the ball. The solution was to simply stick to proper execution, keep his shoulders down, and make sure to extend his follow-through right to the catcher's glove. *Just finish your throw*, he told himself. Now he had a plan to manage any errant thoughts if his focus drifted again in the future. He made it to the World Series the next year and performed like his sensational self! Feeling confident is powerful, but it doesn't ensure you will automatically focus on what you are supposed to be doing when you need to be doing it.

Confidence crushers

You don't need confidence to perform at your best, but that doesn't mean confidence isn't worth working on. Focusing on what you need to do in those big-pressure moments helps get around the need for confidence— and as with Max, confidence can even get in the way! But, when preparing for those big moments, it's useful to recognize why your confidence may slip.

Loose or avoidant thinking makes it harder to get to your best. One of these confidence crushers may be the source of stress that is messing with your success.

FORGET PERFECT

Are you driven to appear flawless? When things don't go your way, or when you make a mistake, do you get mad and just want the performance to be over with? Do you punish yourself with self-criticism or find it hard to enjoy your accomplishments? Maybe you can't even see what you have achieved.

You need to know that there is no clear link between trying to be perfect and performance success. You also need to know that perfection is unattainable and that striving for it is a script for self-defeat.

Mitchell retired as a fifty-something after a very successful and prosperous consulting career. He was precise, liked to feel in control, and coveted personal success. He had become self-consciously overweight and unfit, so he finally booked that all-day executive medical assessment he had been postponing for two years. His approach to the exercise stress test is what caught my attention. He was there to get healthy, yet he voluntarily quit the treadmill test as soon as it got tough. He joked that there was no point in trying to do his best because then he would be expected to do even better the next year, so he might as well leave room for improvement. It was clear Mitchell knew he would perform poorly on the test so his attitude was "If I can't be good at this, then I am not going to try." He soothed his feelings of inadequacy at the expense of his health.

The other side of perfectionism is having trouble seeing how good you are. I sat down for lunch with a client in a vibey Beverly Hills bistro. I hadn't seen Daisy in person for some time, since she was guest starring on a TV show. She was a little down: "I feel like I am in a slump. I am doing some of my best work on self-tapes but not getting the jobs. Do you think if I sent you two tapes you'd be able to see if there's something I'm missing in my game?" I am no acting coach so I knew she was really asking if I could detect any performance glitches driven by her perfectionistic tendencies. She wondered if she was showing tension or hesitation or appearing rushed. She was worried she wasn't good enough.

Daisy has made regular and guest-star appearances in many TV series, has written, directed, and produced, and been in hit Hollywood movies. She has been making a constant living as a professional actor for decades. She was doing great, but like most perfectionists she tended to forget this when stressed. She wanted more, which is fine, but she couldn't see what she had already accomplished. And it was interfering with her self-assurance.

Halfway through our conversation (and very delicious pasta), Daisy's phone lit up. "I'm sorry but I have to answer this, my agent doesn't call to chitchat." She'd just got the part in a medical drama, and she needed to get to the set right away. We both burst with excitement. Off she went to this new opportunity while I happily lingered over the rest of my meal and her success. Things were back in line. Daisy wasn't in a slump; she had just been impatient and self-critical while wading through uncertainty.

If your tendency toward perfection is undermining your achievement or your self-worth, ask yourself to be reasonable. After all, you can't control everything even if you think you should be able to! When it is time to perform, try aiming for excellence or even good enough so you can move away from how you feel and restore your attention to what you need to do.

EXCUSES ARE EASY

We all make excuses from time to time, but some people are fierce in their self-deception and their need to justify in the face of defeat. "It's not my fault. No one told me what to do," "I didn't get enough sleep last night," "I work so hard, I deserve better results," "Of course I got a lousy mark, that teacher never explains anything," "I just don't have time to eat properly." You get the idea.

Sometimes it's easier for others to spot our excuses for us. Zac was a former athlete turned triathlon dad. He was competing well in his age group, so he decided to challenge himself and enter a higher-level event. Zac described this tougher race as going great until he made the transition to the final leg. As he was starting his run, he reached for his last energy gels, realizing that he had inadvertently dumped them out of the back of his shirt when he hopped off his bike. He was lamenting that he would have run much better if he had been able to fuel up on the way to the finish when his wife cut him off. She too was a competitor and knew what he was capable of. She calmly reminded him, "You train hard all the time without gels and for longer periods, why didn't you just gut it out like you usually do?" Even Zac could see the truth. When he dropped his gels, he dropped his focus too. By panicking about being slow he'd disconnected from his pace and stride, which made him slow. He wanted a reason why he didn't finish strong, so he put full blame on the gels. Sometimes we need someone to gently challenge us to drop the excuses to help us move forward.

WIGGLING

Excuses help us avoid facing hard truths, but what if what we're avoiding isn't a truth at all? What if we're just scared to face a possibility? That's where wiggling comes in.

Returning from a difficult injury is never easy, but Wren, a pro tennis player, knew exactly what she had to do to get back on tour: regain a consistent backhand. She knew she needed to hit up and out on the ball but kept bailing at the last moment. Her backhand was wild, and she wanted to know why.

Exploring the situation with her was not easy as she kept wiggling away from talking about what was obstructing her. She wanted to get her career back but was avoiding and ignoring any discussion of how to get it there. Wren was smart and usually objective, but her wiggle factor was on overdrive—the persistent avoidance of an issue. With patience and time from both of us, she finally wiggled herself into a corner. She had no option but to reveal her nagging worry, that due to injury and time off, she may no longer be good enough to get her ranking back. She was unintentionally botching her shot to protect herself; she did not want to find out that her career may be over. Once she understood what she was doing and why, she got back to her efficient on-court focus. After a year away, she was back on tour, and her backhand was better than ever.

TINKERING

Do you tinker with an already good plan but end up wishing you left well enough alone? I walked into a beautiful reception area quietly bustling with chicly dressed staff. It was so snazzy and glitzy that for a moment I thought I was in the wrong place, not in a medical clinic. I was meeting a cosmetic surgeon to observe him in the operating room and to talk performance, including his personal preparation strategies and how he best communicated with staff and patients.

It was a fascinating morning, but it was his perspective on fiddling too much that really stuck with me, as he had seriously good advice. When preparing a patient for eyelid surgery, once he marks his incision lines with a felt pen, he spends extra time (lots of it) confirming and reconfirming his measurements so that he is not tempted to tweak and change the markings during the surgery. The last thing he wants is to remove too much skin and leave his patient with that surprised look. He said if you don't put in the time to do the preparation, it is easy to doubt and then alter things in the moment. "Don't tinker, always trust your markings."

I DON'T DESERVE IT

One winter I arrived in the lobby of a hotel tucked away in the Alps to be greeted by a team coach and trainer. They told me to check in and then go straight to Carly's room, as she was waiting for me. I had an idea what I would find as this was a world championship skiing competition and emotions would be combustible if not already on fire.

Carly had been shut away in her room all day, overwhelmed with her desire to win a world title later that week. As her anxieties rose so did her frustrations. How could she be expected to perform with a suddenly tender back, along with the lack of attention from the training staff, and what about those loud, irritating teammates? After having the chance to unburden her frustrations, she confessed that she wasn't confident she would win. Her self-honesty allowed us to look for a more productive approach to her upcoming races.

She had been thinking often about her competitors, that they were better, that this win would happen for them but not for her. So we started to look at the facts. She knew she was as good, that she had won and been on the podium at world-level competitions before, and that her recent races and training were on point. So I asked her, "Why not you?" She had no answer for me. She had been caught up in her emotions rather than what she had to pay attention to while on the course. She was able to calm down and shift her thoughts from "It will be someone else" to "Why not me?" This strategy allowed her to tone down the voice that loudly insisted other athletes were more deserving than she, to hear the one that told her body what to do in the tougher sections of the course in order to win.

It was a thrilling trip to the top of the podium, even in the absence of easy confidence. Check in with yourself to make sure you aren't handing victory to someone else for no reason. Ask yourself, "Why not me?"

SLUMPY STUFF

Have you ever scanned the bench of a hockey team (or any team) that just got scored on in a close or important game? Slumped shoulders, heads down, and silence between players are what you are likely to see. These behaviors are indications that their resilience may be waning and that they may have trouble recovering from a setback.

Slumpy stuff shows up everywhere. I was talking with a young PhD student about her upcoming committee meeting. She had to present her research proposal to a panel of professors and was on edge. Her biggest worry was not being able to answer all their inevitable and esoteric questions that, let's face it, can be hard to answer and even understand when you are just starting out. Due to her supervisor's illness that week, the meeting was changed from in person to online. Now she was unnerved. She preferred to present in person. This surprised me as many people feel less vulnerable behind a screen in their own homes.

Curious, I asked her to explain. "If I can't answer a question fully, I am worried they will think I am stupid and be hard on me. (This was her tension talking, not her intellect.) I feel like they will be less hard on me in person." This was a new perspective for me.

She was concerned that they wouldn't be able to see her face as clearly on-screen as they could in person. As such, they wouldn't know when she was uncomfortable or unsure and would unreasonably press her with difficult questions. She counted on using her body language to indicate when she wanted them to back off. In essence, she was trying to protect herself by influencing their behavior.

This approach had to go. She was so busy thinking about how to avoid difficult questions and a poor performance that she diverted her attention from giving her best answers. We talked about how she couldn't count on trying to control their behavior. If they decided to be tough, so be it. Her best results (and feelings) would come from staying calmer and connecting to her material and her answers. Besides, looking and acting disengaged may invite more questions. She was much better off trying to sit tall and look composed as it would not only help her feel less wound up but would indicate to her professors that she was capable and doing her best.

We know it is easier to change our behavior than to try to change how we feel, so start behaving with confidence. This is a tactic that makes a real difference to how you feel and how others perceive you. It's not about faking confidence per se but about nudging yourself out of feeling down and done.

Watch your posture. Keep your head up, your shoulders down, and your face loose. Breathe a little slower, exhale a little longer. Shake yourself out. When you meet someone new, look up and smile a little. On the golf course, or heading into a meeting, walk with purpose and energy. In class, ask that question with a firm, clear voice. Take the time for easy small talk here and there or for a casual conversation when you are tense. Acting confident has a surprisingly quick and significant effect on how you feel. It will help you relax and engage, as well as show others that you are in control of your emotions and ready to perform.

Forget the slumpy stuff, stand tall and stay in there. You will feel better, act better, be perceived in a more positive light, and even lift those around you.

The confidence solution

Confidence is great. It feels positive and sets you up for a more relaxed and automatic performance. In short, having confidence makes it easier for you to get to your best. But feeling confident isn't enough because success depends on what you do, not on how you feel. Don't get me wrong, thinking *I feel good, I've got this* is an excellent and constructive way to start your performance, but don't stop there. Do you know how to quickly restore your attention to the task, should you need to? Or do you just wing it and hope for the best? I want you to be ready for any distraction or obstacle that could derail you, or your confidence, in the moment.

The solution to managing confidence, whether it's low or high, is much the same as solutions to other problems outlined in this book: Focus on what to *do*. Have a backup plan that doesn't rely on how you feel. Preplan one or two cues to keep you connected to the momentary task or that reconnect you if you drift. If you are a grand prix show jumper you may need to tell yourself to keep your "eyes up" to maintain direction in the ring and balance on your horse. Maybe the next time you accidentally hit the ball into the net rather than over it, you decide to keep your mouth shut and your racquet in your hand, so you don't ramp up your frustration and flub your match. During your upcoming job interview, perhaps you will choose to relax into your chair and speak slower. Whatever your next performance, don't make the mistake of searching for confidence rather than focusing on competence. Performing well leads to confidence, not the other way around.

Kristen, the *American Idol* singer at the start of this chapter, did just that. She buckled down and worked to move away from her feelings of worry onto what she needed to do. The judges were blown away by her next auditions and told her she had a chance not only at the top ten but to win. As she prepared for her final performances, Kristen kept working to manage her overthinking and self-doubts. Now when she starts to go on about confidence, she stops herself and says, "Okay, I know it's overrated, just breathe, connect to the song, and stay on top of those high notes." Maybe she'll win, maybe she won't (that's life), but a confidence issue won't be the deciding factor.

Chapter Five

You Can't Outsource Your Own Motivation

People think my job is to motivate others, or to give inspirational pep talks. It's not, and I don't. In truth, I find motivation to be an annoying and deceptive topic. Motivation is one of those big concepts that people cling to as if it is the secret ingredient to peerless performance and life success. "If you are motivated you can do anything and conquer any obstacle," we are told. I don't see it this way.

One can be highly motivated without any hope of success. You may dream of being an astronaut but not have the slightest knack for science, technology, engineering, or mathematics (STEM). Likewise, effort with no strong motivation can still garner great results, much pleasure, and true satisfaction. You may love being a musician but be unwilling to devote the time necessary to be truly great. This is a reasonable choice, not a personal failure.

Motivation won't make you better on its own. It is not a cure-all and it won't solve your performance problems, so I don't spend much time talking about it with clients. What we do talk about is how to get past it to achieve results.

My clients walk through the door motivated. They want something—to gain success or avoid failure. Just like you. They are motivated by different situations, styles, feedback, attitudes, challenges, opportunities, and results. And just like anyone, they let obstacles block what they are motivated to get. So, we look at their psychological barriers to inspired performance and plan a good work-around. Which you can too.

I can't give you motivation, no one can. But let's take a moment to talk about it because it's important to understand what motivation is or isn't, and what it can or can't do for us.

Motivation is a desire, a want. It is an indication of how driven you feel to make something happen. But *feeling* motivated doesn't mean you will act. This is where motivation trips people up and gets in the way of results:

*   I am *so* motivated to beat him.
*   I really don't want to lose.
*   You don't look like you want it, you need to show that you are motivated out there!
*   She humiliated me, I will show her.
*   I am motivated to be the best.

All these urgent and powerful feelings may be real, but if left to flow freely they will distract you from acting with focus in the moment and work against you. I prefer to hear:

*   I am *so* motivated to stay calm when things get rough or when I am not getting my way.
*   Of course I don't want to lose, so I am really motivated to stay focused on trying to keep my form.
*   You don't look like you are trying out there, are you frustrated? Or did I get that wrong?
*   She behaved badly—I don't have to do the same.
*   I want to get the most out of myself and hit my top gear, whatever that is. I would like to find out how far I can go as I think it might be pretty far.

This version of the same motivations indicates that you understand the difference between wanting something and knowing how to make it happen.

You can be motivated all day long but if you don't move beyond the desire for results and onto focusing on what to do, your motivations will be ineffective; they could even stop your progress entirely. Being motivated isn't enough. You have to know what gets in the way.

Where does motivation come from?

As I said, other people can't give you motivation, but that doesn't stop them from trying. Way back when, during my first year of university, our field hockey national team coach thought she would try. It didn't go well.

We had been training together for six months, five hours a day, each of us hoping to make the final cut and play at the world field hockey championships. A month before the final selections the coach decided to raise the stakes. At the end of each practice after drills and skills and sprinting and scrimmaging, before we all went our separate ways in the afternoon to classes or jobs, we had to play a new game she had devised: Grits. (I have no clue why it was called that.) It was a game of field hockey but played in a much smaller space with no rules and no umpires. The coach wanted to motivate us. She wanted us to compete even harder and prove to her how much we wanted a spot on that team. Every one of us wanted a spot and we understood that selection required a good showing in this inane game.

At first it was fun. People were respectful, we called our own fouls, and were good sports and teammates. Then the coach insisted we scrap our self-imposed honor system (which had kept us in check) and play through all infractions, whether intentional or accidental.

People became angry with the game and each other. Then the coach shipped in a few additional players from across the country who she said were also eligible for selection and could bump any of us originals off the roster. Players turned on each other and went into survival mode. There was yelling, hacking, cheating, and injuries. A former team member recently recounted the day that another player "flattened" her. When she looked skyward, from her new position on her back, that teammate was standing over her, glaring, and holding her stick in an intimidating way. The more this ridiculous coach *motivated* us, the more chaos prevailed. It was stunning. It was mayhem.

In a matter of weeks the performance culture we had built over months had disintegrated. The hockey was terrible, and we had lost our good team vibe. Nobody benefited from this "motivational" experiment. To this day there are difficult memories (and some palpable trauma) shared by those who didn't make the team and those of us who did. I am all for helping people learn to toughen up in the face of pressure but that is just it, you must *help* them (or yourself). Help them figure out their own barriers to high performance so they can perform and contribute their best. Don't purposefully drop the barriers in front of them just to see what happens.

So where does motivation come from? Everyone on that team was motivated, and everyone had their own reasons for training, playing, and putting up with things that would now be termed maltreatment (at the least). Motivation comes from you, and only you can decide how motivated you are.

How do you use motivation?

While motivation has to come from within, sometimes we need a little kick-start.

A university field hockey player told me how mad she was during a game when her coach subbed her out. She was the best on the team and playing okay, but she got yanked anyway. Her coach didn't bother to give her any feedback about why he replaced her, and she was irked. But her time-out did her a favor. It forced her to think about her play, what was good or not good enough.

She realized that she knew what to do on the field, she just hadn't done it, and now she found herself on the sidelines, fuming. Fortunately, the coach soon put her back in, handing her a renewed opportunity to manage her performance and show her stuff. She ripped it up. She carried the ball, she was hard on tackles, she created scoring chances. And she made her teammates better. She could have done that right from the start of the game, but she wasn't ready. She had assumed her desire to play well would automatically dial her in. She learned that she had to put her motivation to work, or she would be sitting with it on the bench, sipping water.

This player needed a shake-up and her coach gave her one. I always prefer those in charge to tell someone why they are out or what they have to do to get back in, but the player relied on herself, which is the independence I love to see! Feedback from others is useful and necessary but be ready to motivate yourself.

Sometimes people need more of a jolt to figure out how to act on their motivation, to move beyond their feelings. At a professional baseball game I was sitting quietly in the dugout, chewing lots of really good bubble gum, and watching an implosion. The starting pitcher was having a very bad day, so the manager called it. He walked to the mound and took the ball out of the pitcher's glove. It was only the top of the third inning. The pitcher didn't want to go like this, especially in front of an entire stadium, but he knew it was time. He slumped off the field and down the stairs into the dugout, where he paced up and down a few times, everybody giving him space.

The third time he walked by me I caught his eye. He stopped and plopped down beside me and my bucket of gum. I knew how upset he would be but the tears in his eyes said it all. "My command is shit. I don't know what is happening. My fastball is all over the place. My curveball is my jam and I can't count on it." He wanted it so badly, to break through and be an MLB starter of consistency, of substance. He had it in his sight. He just hadn't anticipated that he would have to dig a little deeper. He wiped his eyes and we resolved to figure it out the next day.

As soon as we sat down for lunch, he lost it. Tears. It happens more than you think. Sometimes a little for me too. So we started to work the problem. We blew right by any talk of motivation and went to the important part of the story, his poor results and why it was happening. He hadn't thought through the steps necessary to pull himself through a poor showing. He knew how he wanted to feel on the mound, but he didn't know what to do when he felt big pressure and the mistakes were mounting.

We brought it all back to how he got there in the first place. What made him great? What was happening on the mound when he was strong? What did he have to do on the mound to make it work for him? Once we talked about his pitching strengths and his many previous in-game successes, he started to relax. Then he was able to talk me through how to throw his money pitches and how to improve his other ones. He drilled down to the few things that would make a difference to his execution when things got tough or would keep them from getting tough. He left our meeting with written reminders of what he had to do when he felt the inevitable pressure of his own motivation.

We weren't done yet. We needed to talk again to review his thoughts, add and edit to solidify his approach and make it start to stick. We took another shot at it the next day hanging out on the field before he went to warm up with long toss. (It is amazing how far and hard they can *toss* a ball.) We reiterated the importance of working to shift his focus when he felt pressure, which could be during every pitch.

Over the remaining three months of the season we talked a little and texted a lot. He would rate his performance out of 10 and tell me what was good, not so good, and what (if anything) he was going to adjust for his next outing. We talked about his stats, and he told me about the situations he pitched his way into and out of. He got comfortable with strategies like breathing and talking to himself. (These are all laid out in part two.) He was now loose and throwing the ball his way. He cured his performance troubles because he learned to shift his focus away from motivation in the moment. No more tears.

His coach or teammates could have easily written off his poor performances as lack of motivation. I assure you unmotivated people don't cry when they talk about achieving their goals. Because he was motivated to improve, he was willing to look at what he had previously resisted: his mental approach. The solution had nothing to do with how hard he was working, either. He had to learn to work better.

Thankfully, his teammates were supportive, but it is easy to make assumptions about other people's motivation. Does any of this sound like you?

* She doesn't look like she enjoys playing, I don't think she really wants this.
* If he were more motivated, he would do what I say.
* He is lazy, he is only motivated to do the easy stuff.
* Even though she is injured she should be back playing by now, she just isn't motivated to be number one.

I try to mute this attitude when I hear it. When assessing another's motivation level, please watch your personal biases. A golf coach kept telling me about a player's motivation. "You can tell she doesn't want this." Surprised, I asked why he would say that. "She gets mad when she misses, she is always talking about a tight shoulder or an aching knee, her parents are always complaining, and she doesn't seem like she wants to get better. Don't you think so, Dana?"

No, I didn't. It's not unusual to get mad at our mistakes. Injuries are not uncommon when you train and compete as a young professional. Her parents complaining was not her fault. And what pro doesn't want to get better?

"I don't see that," I said. "Whenever I have spoken with her, she is determined to be good, she can get wound up about results, but she is working to be able to calm down on the course. She definitely wants it, but she is uncertain at times. She gets scared of her expectations and is trying to figure out how to shift her focus around that."

His response: "Why would she be scared?" I was incredulous. He had played on the PGA Tour and knew how it felt to be worried about not performing well.

But then I got it. The real issue was that he couldn't find a way to get her to hear him. He was impatient with her progress and unsure how to guide her further, so he blamed her. He wanted to move on when it got tough, to coach other players he thought would be easier to help advance. He stopped giving her regular feedback on her game, and even pulled back from his usual chitchat with her.

The solution? Ask. Talk. Have a direct conversation. The truth was this player did everything to get better, but the coach chose to see her frustration as a lack of motivation. He stopped taking an interest. He didn't want to work at it as failing with her would reflect poorly on him. So he divested himself.

People can support and encourage you, absolutely. (I get to do this all day long and love to be a part of it.) Should people challenge you and hold you accountable? Definitely. Can they help you when you blow it? My goodness yes, we all need that. But to be responsible for your motivation to act? To force you to want something? No, that is yours and only yours. You must look inward and find what is in the way. You can't outsource your own motivation.

Some people have no problems being clear about their motivations. I spoke with Cooper about his diagnosis with Parkinson's, a progressive nervous system disorder that affects movement in the form of tremors, stiffness, and slowness. There is no known cure. Cooper quickly determined that the critical factor in slowing the progression of his symptoms was exercise. It was a daunting task, but he would have to force himself to work out daily if he wanted to maintain his declining but relatively good health.

He needed a set of strategies to help him stick to his various exercise routines and he liked the idea of using performance psychology. He started each day with a few minutes of breathing and "seeing" himself in the gym lifting weights with purpose, ease, and strength. He would also see himself improving with extra repetitions or increased weight. During the day he liked to daydream about his symptoms slowing and reversing; in his mind he would walk smoothly and even go for a short run with an athletic stride. Daydreaming is actually a useful skill when done purposefully, something we'll look at closely in chapter 15. He used short bursts of images not just to get himself into the gym but to buoy his emotional functioning and self-regard.

"Illness robs you of the body, but it also erodes your sense of dignity. I see being ill with dignity as the parallel to performance in athletics. You do your best in sports to win, ideally with grace, and with illness you do your best to prevail. But prevailing does not mean just surviving, although that is clearly part of it. I see prevailing as sustaining your sense of dignity however you can." Showing up for himself daily slowed Cooper's symptoms and preserved his dignity. We developed strategies together to keep him on task, but only he could do this for himself.

Most people I talk to are motivated to be spectacular. This is an excellent motivation: go big and try to get it. But, as with Cooper, a person's particular *spectacular* may look different.

A professional hockey client said, "As a rookie last year I got called up and played a bunch of games in the NHL but this season I want to make the big team right out of training camp." We both knew what he was motivated to do, so now we could discuss how to do it. After assessing him we decided that he was naturally a passive, more hesitant person. He could also get caught up in what the coach or his dad would think about his play. He was worried about mistakes and criticism. We discussed these relevant motivations and he decided his most significant need was to be more physical during the game.

He was motivated to do this so he changed his pregame preparation to include bringing his tension down so he could feel loose and then run some highlight images in his head seeing himself playing hard. He had to warm up with greater intensity to make sure he was ready to initiate body contact and finish his checks. He also planned reminders to go over when he was on the bench between shifts, to keep him connected to the game.

His particular spectacular wasn't about setting scoring records or being an all-star, he just wanted to make the team. He couldn't control if that would happen or if he would start the season with the farm team, but he didn't sit on his motivations. He moved beyond his desires onto doing the one thing that would make him ready to do his best. This approach leads to results and satisfaction. Great work.

Define your motivations and then busy yourself with what may get in the way so you can work around any glitches. One of the bright young female tennis prospects I work with put it so very well: "I don't like to overdo thinking about all that stuff, it weighs me down a bit. I like to think about what the season could bring (read *be spectacular*) and let it flow into existence. I think about what I want in general but I don't force it, I like a softer focus. For instance, this year I see myself acting like the professional women do, calm and composed, not showing negative emotion when they struggle or make a mistake. Also, I want to improve my forehand and serve, and know the best way to do this is to focus more on my performance cues during practice." That's it. Simple, not too much, self-directed, self-motivated. Awesome approach.

Motivation is easy to hide behind. A middle-distance runner had been having a good season but felt he could be getting better results. "I am running well but not all the way to the finish." He was consistent but too comfortable. He ran half the race well and then started to get distracted by his good running. "I want podiums. I know I can do it. I have everything I need to be able to do it, but I am mentally holding back, I can feel it."

"What if you don't get a podium this season?" He was surprised by my question, and I think a little offended that I would mention this possibility.

"That would not be good."

"How would you do if you raced the whole race, not just part of it?"

"I would be on the podium."

"Can anybody be on the podium if they are only racing half a race?"

"Well, no, not at this level."

"So, you have to run it properly, and push it more, to focus on your relaxed form to the finish?"

I wasn't being unkind. I wanted to tease out the reason for his lack of urgency. "What are you thinking about going into the race day?"

It didn't take him long to say, "Things like, I don't have to do it today, I can do it another day, there is always the next race." His attitude was too cautious and low pressure. His desire to be *spectacular* was high but his lack of resolve to push in the moment undercut his ability.

Ultimately, he decided to "run it right." His results came when he stepped out from behind his motivations.

When motivation isn't there

What if you aren't motivated? Chatting over smoothies (him) and coffee (me) at the team breakfast on game day, an NFL player wanted to talk about getting more from himself on the field. "I am playing fine, but my motivation has been slipping the last few weeks." He was starting games and had good stats so this didn't add up. He couldn't explain what was going on. "I never thought about it before. I have always felt motivated, so my current attitude is bugging me. But I am older, I have made good money over the years, I have done this for a long time, I have a family now, and I am very grateful for my situation so maybe I am just not motivated anymore."

What? You aren't motivated to be your great self? You don't mind not playing the way you always have and know you still can? What are you worried about? What is in the way?

He said, "I am not making splash plays and I am not feeling good about it." Now we were on the right track.

"Maybe you think these splash plays should just happen? You are all titans of the universe out there and nothing is just going to fall in your lap consistently. You are drifting away from doing what you need to do to make these plays. So why not decide now what you are going to do about it starting with this game? Remember, it only takes one excellent play and you will be back feeling motivated and reengaged."

He seemed to understand that I was gently calling him on his *fears*. He played better after that but still no splash plays. We spoke again the next week and the first thing out of his mouth was "I have decided to be good for these last six games. Before each play I am going to tell myself to breathe and be good." He was on it. He had shut me right up. I had nothing to say but "Go do it!" He splashed big that game.

But we weren't done. Before the next game we spoke again. I could hear water jets fizzing in the background as he hopped into the hot tub in the training room. He was relaxed and happy with his play but still felt he could do more. I asked for specifics. He had evaluated his game and was ready with a response. "I didn't start the way I wanted to. My *mentals* were teetering, I wasn't locked all the way in. I got pushed off my mental routine. . . . I got hit hard and bruised my kneecap. I was distracted and feeling a little sorry for myself and then made a mistake. But I got it together for the second half. I thought about it at halftime and decided I needed to get my focus back to playing hard. I reminded myself to do my thing, to breathe and get back to my mental routine for each play." His response on the field was even better this time. His adjustments for the next game were to check in with himself after every quarter and during TV time-outs to make sure he was focused on playing hard. To not let his *feels* dictate his play, to make his skills run the show.

His motivation, which had initially lagged, was resoundingly restored by holding himself accountable for every play. He upgraded his performance, improved his stats, his coaches noticed, and he felt motivated to go for more. He performed game after game. What a great way for him to finish out the season and be primed for the playoffs.

Can you suddenly lose your motivation? Is it possible that you just don't want it anymore? Perhaps, but this is rare. More likely your decelerated drive is trying to tell you something and it could be important.

During the first week of his first spring training a player sat down across from me in a conference room and said, "I am not motivated to play anymore. I think I am done." I had spoken to this freshly drafted athlete a couple of times during the previous month and hadn't heard any hint of a motivation crisis. I had only heard excited anticipation for the upcoming preseason.

When I asked what his change of mind was due to, he couldn't tell me. He just felt lackluster about getting on the field. I knew how skilled he was and also how self-critical, so I was immediately skeptical of his new mood. From our calls I knew how he wanted to prove himself, especially to others, people like his successful father and his new coaches. He was finally here, ready to go, but he was completely backing off.

He wanted to give up entirely, but I wouldn't let him. Not until we peeled back his motivation to see what he was concealing. He was deep in self-preservation mode—he wanted to escape the pressure of his own expectations and avoid "being a failure." He needed a plausible excuse, one that others would accept as legitimate and not his responsibility. Motivation was the perfect out. How could he be expected to force himself to conjure enthusiasm if it just wasn't there? How could he be a failure if motivation eluded him, not his abilities? The pressure to perform at spring training was derailing him. Motivation, not a lack of it, was getting in his way. All he needed was to understand this so he could accept it and move past it, back to himself.

In this case, a supposed lack of motivation was an excuse, but sometimes it can be a big helpful stop sign, and it's crucial to know the difference. I was talking to the talented students at the Royal Conservatory of Music about performing under the pressure that they had already faced and would inevitably continue to face, and ended up telling them about the happiest day of my childhood. My wonderful mother had finally let me quit piano lessons! I have nothing but respect for those stylish and elegant concert pianists, but it wasn't going to happen for me. That would require at least some aptitude. My recollection is that I was required to do something I had zero drive for. Not only was I completely uninterested and disengaged, but more poignantly, I was lousy. I was not motivated to be spectacular or anything close to that. In such situations why not move on? And sooner rather than later so you can invest time and energy into trying something that may delight you.

Luckily, they laughed at my ten-year-old self and knew of course that I wasn't telling them to quit; I was trying to highlight that what they do is hard. Motivation is tricky because it can be a great excuse to avoid trying, or for dodging possible failure. But it can also tell you that something is in your way or that you need to stop and change direction. You have to scrutinize feelings to find out what a lack of motivation is truly telling you. Don't wait for a poor performance or an outside appraisal to get it right. Your motivation is yours, and yours only. Make it work for you!

Motivation is a desire, not a reliable strategy for getting results. Motivated or not, performing is about getting beyond *wanting* it to focusing on *doing* it.

Chapter Six

Superstitions Aren't Super

"Where is my red hat? Who took it? I can't play without my red hat!" Jaden was frantically scrabbling around the back of the van. She was desperate to find her well-worn, grubby, but "lucky" hat before her tee time. She was about to play her first professional tournament and her nerves were showing.

I had expected Jaden to be anxious (who wouldn't be?), but she was beginning to unravel more than I had anticipated. I nonchalantly suggested she wear the red hat that she had just pulled out of her bag, the one she was holding in her hand. I knew the answer I would get, but I decided to risk it anyway. Sure enough, she snapped her head up, dug her eyes into me, and said, "You know, I have never worn this one before, look at it, it is brand new! It won't help me play well at all!" We had two hours to pull her head out of her hat and get it back into her game.

Even though superstitions are irrational and silly and, most importantly, have nothing to do with skilled performance, I have come across many.

A Major League Soccer player told me that he was advised by a mental-skills consultant to chew gum during a game to lock in his focus. How does that work? He said it didn't. Other clients have tried to stop negative thoughts by snapping a rubber band on their wrist each time they noticed that an errant notion had weaseled its way into their consciousness. Some people believe this, or something like it, works. Again, I am not sure how this is helpful.

Some athletes *have* to tap the sides or top of their dressing or locker room doorframe, in a certain order, before stepping out to play. And if they mess it up, they have to go back and do it again. (This one is not uncommon.)

Another client, an Olympic open water swimmer, shared in a light moment that she hates seaweed, hates fish near her, and is more comfortable in a pool. When competing out in the oceans of the world, she doesn't look down for fear of seeing fish. She doesn't like going to the beach or wading into the water because of the fish. She is superstitious the night before a race and will not eat any kind of fish so they are not tempted to eat her the next day. This way she "stays with the pack and will be safe." This was unique.

To secure a good performance, some clients talk about eating the same meals every game day, no variations allowed. Or put their socks on in the same order for the entire playoff run. Another Olympic client once regaled me with a seriously ridiculous superstition. A team consultant had recommended to him that he urinate in the pool before a competition to claim secret dominance of his territory. Yikes. We laughed. (He never did it.)

Superstitions keep your tension flowing and your focus off task. They are anxiety driven, not based on reason or knowledge. A superstition is an unjustified belief that a random action, by you or someone or something else, will bring luck or prevent disaster. People turn to superstitions when they lack confidence or feel insecure or threatened. Acting out a superstition may offer the illusion of control over outer conditions but in reality is not connected to your ability to perform well.

Superstitions can conveniently blur the line between self-control and out-of-my-control. An actor I worked with was certain he would not get a callback for an audition if the casting director didn't smile at him when he first walked into the room. In his mind, a welcoming gesture invited him to relax, rely on his preparation, and connect to his lines. Whereas a neutral greeting, which he interpreted as disinterest, confirmed his deepest worry that he wasn't good enough (even though he had current and upcoming projects booked). This way he could surrender mental control. Someone else's actions absolved him from having to fight to manage his tension and his mental chatter. It was out of his hands, what could he do?

Superstitions are an indicator of how anxious and distracted you are. It's far better to use tangible coping strategies to calm a turbulent mind and restore attention to the task. Learn how to count on yourself, not on a smile offered by a stranger.

How superstitions keep you down

Superstitions may be part of your strategy to perform well. Let's look at why they shouldn't be. I had just done a Zoom talk for a university's athletes and alumni. A few days later, I received a note from Brooke, who had been on the call. An avid golfer, she said my talk had already helped her to her lowest score ever. I am always pleased to hear about people's improvements and successes of course, but then she got to the interesting part. I had spoken about superstitions in that talk and Brooke mentioned that they are a big part of her strategy. For example, when she had her best game ever she wore a different sports bra, which is now the only one she'll wear. Also, the logo on the ball had to be turned a certain way, and so on.

I chuckled at the bra thing and noted that she could certainly keep wearing it, and keep her other superstitions going too, but they really had nothing to do with her success. I continued: "It may be more helpful to remind yourself to slow down and breathe as you are preparing for your shot." Regarding an issue she brought up about sand traps (such a normal distraction), I commented that perhaps she could remember to pick a small target, make sure to have a slow takeaway, and most importantly, hit through the ball so she finished high. Seems obvious, but it was worth reminding her that it is better to think of the correct target. If you keep thinking about the sand trap it is funny how you can make the ball go there. "And this way," I added, "you won't be squandering your focus on your super bra . . . lol."

The next day, Brooke wrote back exclaiming that she'd played even better! She made an immediate improvement in her game when she learned to shift her attention from pointless, effort-wasting superstitions to execution: what she was going to do from shot to shot.

If superstitions are so unproductive, why do people succumb to them? Superstitions are seen as a way to cope with the tension and anxiety you feel when faced with uncertainty. One will grasp at a superstition to help soothe the fear around results. Wearing your prized Ivy League university ring to your final exams may be a "power" reminder that you are a capable student, which can make you feel a little less stressed, but your ring is not the difference between achieving a good or bad mark. If the cost of enacting your superstition is low, like turning the logo on your golf ball to the right position, then I won't get in your way. If you can move along quickly and refocus your mind on the real skills that will allow you to perform, then carry on. Just recognize that superstitions are a substitute for the real strategies that will benefit your performance.

Superstitions vs. routines

Superstitions are a big indication that you are anxious, whereas routines are a sequence of specific actions. Routines set you up to execute well and come in all shapes and sizes. They will take you one step closer to your desired performance. Even preparing for a good night's sleep is routine-worthy. For instance, taking the hour before your bedtime to get away from your screens and devices, to cool the temperature of your room, and read a novel (or at least not a work report) can only help you hit the pillow with a quieter mind and the ability to breathe yourself into a restful night.

Routines are a great way to keep your mental chitchat in check and your attention deliberate.

I worked with a mental health advocate who was starting to do a lot of speaking to corporate groups. Her topic was definitely compelling, but she felt that her ability to engage the audience was inconsistent. I asked her to tell me more about her good days and the not-so-good days. On the former, she was relaxed and connected to what she was talking about; on the latter, she felt her delivery was rushed and flat.

I then asked about her pre-talk routine and found out she didn't have one. Prior to taking the stage, she preferred to busy herself with talking to people or any other distraction that took her mind off the sea of expectant faces that would soon be staring up at her. She thought this "just step up and let it happen" attitude was the best way to prevent her from over-thinking and appearing nervous. Upon reflection, she realized that this random and unscripted approach was in fact unreliable and frustrating.

As she continued to describe her last few talks, we discovered that her opening was the key. If she started her opening minute with energy and clarity, she could see the curiosity and encouragement in individual faces and was able to continue with self-assurance right through to her closing comments.

So, we settled on a routine that would ensure a strong start. I wanted her to plan her opening, to set up her story. It was important that she memorize her opening minute so she could grab the audience's attention and not fritter it away with small talk while she got comfortable.

Prior to her introduction, she would take a few minutes for herself to step out of the presentation room into the hallway or walk to the bathroom. The place didn't matter, just the space to do a quick body scan (checking for tension in her face, shoulders, arms, and legs) and take a few slow breaths to loosen any tightness she felt. She would then remind herself that she was good at this. After all, she had been invited here to share her insights. She finished her routine by reminding herself to "speak louder, they need to hear me in the back." A routine for an impactful start allowed her to quickly settle into her story and keep her audience intrigued, making it a satisfying experience for everybody.

Staying connected to your routine

For actions to be effective they have to be deliberate and focused. Routines are no different. While working with an NHL team, I noticed the head coach's pregame routine. He would stand alone in the dressing room, arms at his sides, game notes in hand, looking dead ahead for exactly sixty seconds. He would then deposit said notes in his jacket pocket before purposefully striding out to the bench ready, in his mind, for battle. I was curious about what was going on in his head during this minute. When we talked about it, he admitted that over time this routine, intended to be conscious preparation, had become a set of rote behaviors. He realized that often he was just going through the motions. He felt more ready for the start of the game when he actually used that minute to slow down and remind himself of his key tactics and possible line matchups. He reconnected to making his routine productive rather than just a familiar time filler.

Beyond routines

You have rolled through your pre-event routine. You feel good—more in control and ready to take action. Now what? Just step up and do it? Well, you are not done just yet. It's important to make a smooth transition from your routine to the actual task.

Perhaps you're a golfer. You have decided on the ball path and taken your practice putts, but that doesn't ensure you will automatically execute as intended. Have you ever been well prepared for a putt only to have too many thoughts (or no thoughts at all) interfere at the last second? The moment you make contact with the ball, perhaps you're thinking about the result, jumping ahead to what it will look like if you do or don't sink the putt. You don't intend to, but you lift your head to see where the ball is going mid-stroke, pulling your putter to one side and the ball off line. You were thinking about *how* you were doing, not *what* you were doing.

What is the solution? Like the action plan for confidence in chapter 4, have one or two in-the-moment go-to thoughts to keep you connected to proper execution. For instance, in this situation, just before or during your stroke tell yourself to keep your "head down" or your stroke "long and smooth." If you want the ball to drop into the cup, or at least get closer to it, engage your focus constructively on what you need to do.

Even a second or two between successfully completing your routine and starting the task is plenty of time for an unintentional fleeting thought to derail your focus at the last moment. Decide on a focus point. Connecting to a simple cue that tells your body what to do will keep your mind on track and your execution intact.

Lose your red hat

Routines help you prepare to perform. They provide structure, quality, and consistency to your performance. They organize and minimize your thoughts. They work to lessen tension, prevent errors, and create certainty. Routines are about working with your thoughts, about putting them in order so you are then ready to do your best. They can be loose and casual or precise and more formal. Have a checklist, in your head or written down, so you don't overlook or forget what works for you. You don't have to obediently follow a routine each and every time you execute. Routines can be flexible, depending on the situation. But do guard against absently going through the motions. You must connect to a routine for it to be productive, especially when you feel stressed or distracted.

When you are ready to perform, it is time to shift your focus onto what you are going to do in the moment. At the free-throw line, your pre-shot routine of bouncing the ball three times may allow you to loosen your shoulders (which is good), but you know you still need to get your elbow up if you want to put it through the rim. Watch that this good routine doesn't turn into a bad superstition by forgetting the point is to loosen your shoulders so you can extend your arm—it's not about getting exactly three bounces. The bounces don't matter, the arm extension does.

Jaden, the superstitious golfer from the start of this chapter, never did find her "lucky" hat. Thank goodness, as now she had the opportunity to get serious about strengthening her mental control. We talked through the worst-case scenarios that were surging through her mind so she could declutter her thoughts and clear space to focus on her game. I needed her to be able to consciously connect to the shot in front of her rather than drift ahead to a looming hazard or unintentionally hold back on her signature smooth swing. She settled on a routine that included telling herself to slow down and exhale fully, as well as reminding herself that "it isn't the end of the world." Then she would visualize an "easy swing" before her setup to the ball. There was more but we agreed that these were the important cues for now and it was best to keep it simple at this point. I want to tell you that she won the tournament, but she didn't. However, by pushing herself to keep focused on one shot at a time, she did play well and made the cut in her first pro competition.

Superstitions can invade your preparation—or worse, they can replace it. Superstitions so easily morph into a complex obstacle course, one you have to complete before you even get to the performing part—the important stuff! Don't let your anxieties steal your energy or your focus.

Routines give you a chance to settle and connect to the moment. But they aren't all-powerful and there are no guarantees. To keep your groove out there, prepare to perform. Whether you are walking the course, stepping onto the stage or into the corner office, take a moment to settle, and have a go-to focus point. You may not need it every time but why leave a good performance to chance when you can help make it happen?

Chapter Seven

Bad Advice and Good Communicating

Y ou have heard it all before. Maybe you have even said some of it before. Take a moment and think about all the well-intentioned but lousy performance advice so often dispensed by bosses, coaches, parents, spouses, partners, teachers, coworkers, teammates, or any of us really.

- Just relax out there
- You need to concentrate
- Let the game come to you
- Get mad
- Clear your mind
- Focus harder
- Just go out there and have fun
- Trust yourself
- Don't think about your technique
- Let it happen
- Be aggressive
- Be confident

- Play to win
- Change your attitude
- Don't be afraid to fail
- Eliminate all distractions
- Believe in yourself
- You have to be better than that
- You can't afford to make any more mistakes
- Calm down
- Just walk in there like you own the place
- Don't blow it

The problem with these common comments is that the advice simply doesn't work. While they are meant to encourage a focused performance, they disempower it instead because on their own, they do not advance execution. These types of tips are vague, annoyingly obvious, distracting, critical, or confusing. They are intangible and directionless. What does "focus harder" even mean? I can furrow my brow in concentration and be thinking hard but about the wrong thing. When you are told to "believe in yourself," what if in that moment you don't believe in yourself? Telling someone to "calm down," especially when they are oozing tension, can have the opposite effect, sending someone further into emotional disarray. If you want to have a positive impact on the performance mindset of an individual, or your own, there are better ways.

Turning bad advice into good

In performance situations, those in charge often feel they have to say something but just as often don't know what to say (or how to say it). So they fall back on empty rhetoric that they have heard their bosses say, or what their own coaches told them, or how they were parented themselves. It is easier to pick out what someone shouldn't do or what they are doing wrong than to offer meaningful direction before or after a performance. Having a report plopped down on your desk accompanied only by the comment "This isn't good enough" with no additional information suggesting how to make it better isn't a recipe for excellence or an example of strong leadership. Specific, prescriptive pointers or feedback are performance helpers while descriptive judgments are not.

For example, rather than telling someone to focus, be more specific and remind them of what to focus on. Samantha, a teenage tennis client, turned an erratic serve into a reliable powerhouse by thinking through the feedback she was getting from her coach and taking it one step further. At tournaments her coach would remind her that her serve had to be "more aggressive" if she wanted to win. Which was true. But when Samantha tried to be more aggressive and hit the ball harder, she kept launching it out of bounds. When we talked, I asked Samantha questions about her thoughts and actions before and during her serve. She realized she was trying to generate power from the wrong place. Using her legs for power, not her arm, allowed her to contact the ball higher and accelerate down through the ball to get power and spin. Once she drilled down from her coach's general advice, she was able to focus on what to do to get that accurate "aggressive" serve. The coach needed to go one step further and suggest the specific action that would give her the serve they were both looking for.

Coaches are great but Samantha had a role to play too. She knew what she needed to do once she considered the advice more carefully. Think for yourself and take action. It will add to your performance!

Even when you are trying to be inspiring you can easily miss the mark if you don't follow through on what you say. I worked with an NHL coach during the Stanley Cup playoffs. During team meetings and dinners he kept imploring his players to believe in themselves, to believe they could win, that they *would* win. He said that they couldn't win if they didn't believe they could do it. While I am all for self-belief, in times of stress believing in yourself can be hit-or-miss, and not particularly helpful.

To be effective, this coach needed to provide his players with a solution for gaining or maintaining self-belief rather than just telling them they needed to find it if they didn't have it. Even at this professional level, not every player believed in themselves or that they would be able to overcome pressure and play brilliantly. But every player wanted to win. So why not drill down from a high-level notion to also remind them of what they can do to win? Why not believe in something tangible like your training and preparation? In addition to directing comments to the larger group, he needed to speak to them individually and remind each person of his particular strengths on the ice, or previous good performances and actions that they could repeat.

When communicating on the topic of performance it's easy to make a general pronouncement like "trust yourself" or "relax," but skip it if you can. Go right to the specific content that an individual can *do*. Connect them to the thoughts or actions that will actually make a difference to the quality of their performance—thoughts and actions they can count on. If you make a "don't" comment, that's no problem, just make sure you follow it up with a "do this instead" comment. Think about what you say to your employees, colleagues, students, and children.

"Don't hit the net!" I recently heard a top-level coach advise his player during a big match. The coach was trying to help, of course, but only further distracted an already frustrated player. After all, the player knew he was hitting the ball into the net. Coaches need coaching too, so I leaned over and asked what the player needed to do. "Put more spin on the ball" was the answer. A few quiet minutes passed when I heard, "Get under the ball!" Much better.

Rather than tell your head of business development to "be tougher," follow with specifics. Tell her that underperformance continues on her team because she is avoiding interpersonal conflict. That she must have these hard talks with certain team members in a timely manner to avoid the even harder business of having to fire someone.

Be mindful of what you say to yourself, too. When practicing a new piece of music on your piano or flute, it may be tempting to admonish yourself by saying, "Stop rushing through the piece, watch your tempo." To actually address the issue, you are better off saying, "Slow down, focus on the notes in front of you."

Work to offer quality feedback that will help with taking action. Communicate this way to all your performers, not just the ones you perceive to be better and expect to do well. Remember that with specific prescriptive guidance, your lesser-skilled performers will also have a better opportunity to improve or correct their performance and be better prepared for the next time.

We all have a responsibility when it comes to communication. When you are on the receiving end of feedback or advice, don't be afraid to ask for specifics. When someone blurts out, "Play to win, don't play to lose!" it makes sense to ask for meaningful clarification. I mean, who plays to lose?

What gets in the way of good communication?

Good communication generates better results at work and in life. Natural communicators are able to stay calm and listen to what others are really saying and asking for. The best communicators I have worked with are able to defuse concerns and conflicts quickly. They dig in and look for practical solutions to the issue at hand, they reassure and encourage, and they're not afraid to provide feedback in challenging situations to help people move forward or get back on track.

Good communication is hard work but so very important and worthwhile to get right. Listening openly and expressing yourself clearly invites harmony and productivity. Self-protection and avoiding criticism do not. Defensiveness is the most common communication issue I see and if left unchecked will disrupt relationships and stifle performance. We can all be defensive at times and a little bit here and there is not going to hurt much of anything. But if it becomes a habit and you routinely react to a piece of feedback with anger or ego, or shift blame and fail to take responsibility for your own lapses, you will continue to hold yourself and others down and risk underperforming.

Defensiveness can creep into your communication style without you even being aware of it. I had a Zoom meeting with Maxie and Jackson, the parents of a preteen soccer player. They were smiling but I immediately felt the tension between them. They explained that their daughter, Lauren, had improved greatly over the last year and was now one of the top players on her elite team. Jackson was excited that Lauren had recently been invited to play up an age group while continuing to play a full schedule with her own team. He didn't see any problem with her adding more practice and game days to her already packed weekly schedule. In fact, he thought it was necessary if Lauren wanted to excel to the university or Olympic level. Conversely, Maxie felt strongly that Lauren's new seven-days-a-week soccer commitment was starting to have a negative impact on her overall well-being. She was concerned about Lauren getting enough sleep, having time to do other activities, keeping up with her advanced-level schoolwork, or just having some downtime to do nothing.

Once Maxie and Jackson had each stated their positions, the free-for-all started. Nobody could get a word in, including me. They interrupted and talked over each other, they changed the topic on each other, and they each criticized the other's perspective on what was best for Lauren. Having a real two-way conversation was impossible—it had become a game of who is right and who is going to win this fight.

They were trying to maintain composure but their frustration with each other was quickly closing in on anger. After a few minutes I managed to decipher the undertone of their words so I asked for a pause. I told them honestly what I thought I was hearing. As the "sport expert" in the house, Jackson felt threatened that his knowledge, experience, and advice were being questioned. He was a spectacularly supportive dad but was partly fueled by the praise and attention his daughter's success was earning. Maxie did not feel that her concerns over Lauren's daily well-being were being considered at all. It was clear to all of us that this new super-schedule could push the stress level up for everyone in the family. Maxie felt underappreciated and blown off. Even though they were great partners and supportive parents they had settled into their corners and lost track of trying to find a solution to the issue at hand, which was to help Lauren find a happy balance that would allow her to shine. We had to get this thing back on track!

I gave them some homework. I suggested they talk the situation over with Lauren, but only when they were calm and had preplanned some real options for her to consider. They needed to duke it out ahead of time so they could talk to Lauren as a united front. I did not want Lauren to be unnecessarily exposed to the implicit push-pull between her parents and have to contend with the pressure to please one or the other.

We talked about some basic ground rules for their discussion. Somebody (preferably both) had to stay calm and take responsibility for keeping the discussion on topic. When you feel like interrupting, hold your tongue. Close your mouth and count to five if you have to. Be quiet and listen to the words the other person is saying rather than assuming you have the gist of what they are trying to say. Stop putting your own spin on the words being spoken. Invite the other to continue speaking by saying things like "Go on" or "Tell me more about what you mean," rather than "Yes, but" or "That's ridiculous." And no tantrums allowed!

During our next meeting Maxie and Jackson shared their success. While they still had to remind each other to settle down and let the other finish their comments, they found a solution that worked for everybody. The new schedule shaved a practice or two off Lauren's weekly workload depending on how many games she had during that week. They would try it and make adjustments from there.

Acting defensively causes tension and promotes conflict. Check your own behavior before you assume the other person is the entire problem. Protecting yourself from feeling uncomfortable and threatened, or from viewing yourself in a negative light, can result in you going on the attack and trying to avoid any discussion. In this scenario, your energy is spent on constructing a defense rather than on listening. The danger is that when people don't listen, they hear what they want to and nothing else. They may blame others. They may even attempt to embarrass the other person with put-downs or name-calling. They may yell.

If you use yelling to belittle or "correct" others, or to try to make others obedient to your wants, then you need to find healthy ways to manage your frustration and anger. Yelling for these reasons is always unacceptable, for you and your target. I am not at all suggesting that raised voices are impermissible but there is a difference between yelling and raising your voice. Yelling is condescending and dismissive while a firm voice can be reassuring and supportive. Loud can be good, it just depends on your intention and tone. Clean up your own communication backyard before you start pointing fingers at others and keeping score.

What do good communicators do?

The best communicators are not afraid. They say what they mean and do what they say they are going to do. They are clear and direct and open to discussion. They don't hide their true emotions; they deliver their words considerately. Their intentions are to connect rather than punish. Good communicators believe they have the right to express their needs, wants, and wishes, even when they are angry or distressed. In a conflict situation, they deal with the issues at hand rather than the personality of the other person. They allow ample time for the person with whom they have a problem to express their feelings, and they encourage that person to do so, even when the person is hostile toward them. They understand that body language is important and are careful to sit back and keep their shoulders down. Maintaining an open and approachable demeanor (even if they aren't feeling it) allows the other person to reflect that openness in their own response. They ask open-ended questions rather than assuming they know what the other person meant. They ask for clarification and don't drop their opinion or feedback on someone and then stomp off in rage or victory.

Good communicators focus on finding a solution to the current issue, as the continual rehashing of old issues is unproductive. The really good ones are able keep the future in mind rather than dwelling on what or who caused the conflict in the first place.

Communication can be so destructive. I have heard coaches goad players (male and female) about their weight and the need to lose some of it, ridicule teenagers about their facial blemishes, and privately ask players to rate their teammates' abilities and then expose their answers to those same teammates (a coach did this to me too). At competitions I have heard parents scream in frustration at their children if they lost or didn't think they were trying hard enough or toss expletives at their children's opponents. I have been in the room listening to senior executives criticize the work of employees who are sitting within earshot and have witnessed managers blame colleagues for mistakes of their own making. More than once I've waded into the middle of these situations in an effort to offer more self-aware and responsible ways to communicate, and I'm surprised I've never been fired on the spot!

I have also seen individuals deal with impossible people and difficult situations with generosity and understanding. I have always admired the bosses, parents, teachers, coaches, and colleagues who managed their people by just speaking directly and calmly. They didn't yell and scream, they didn't denigrate, ignore, or make personal comments. They didn't deliver feedback as a joke or make fun of people. And they didn't take criticism personally. What they did was talk about the issue simply and honestly. They said what they wanted to say, not what they were supposed to say, and they were respectful in their delivery. Their words matched their tone. Mistakes and ruptures happen of course, but the best communicators focus on repairing the conflict and reconnecting. No wonder their people trust and work hard for them!

How to do it in the moment

Getting the most out of those around you begins with you. Precise communication creates certainty, strengthens trust, and pushes people to grow and develop. Watch the criticism and catch your defensiveness. Ask yourself, is this person attacking you or just stating a reasonable complaint? Communicate in an uplifting, encouraging way. There is a simple three-step process to connect with your people and find solutions.

BREATHE. Keep your tension down by taking a few slower, deeper breaths and make sure to exhale fully. Drop your shoulders, sit back, and keep your expressions open. Instead of frowning or shaking your head or throwing your hands in the air, maintain eye contact. If you look more approachable (even if you aren't feeling it), the other person will be more likely to discuss the situation more openly. Keep your body language loose and calm. Show attention, forget the fidgeting, looking around, or yawning.

LISTEN LONGER. Connect to the words the other person is saying. Resist the temptation to start formulating your comeback or just placating them with blind acceptance so you can leave. Close your mouth so you don't interrupt unless it is clear they have misconstrued your comments.

ACCEPT. You don't have to agree with the criticism that is being leveled at you, but you will have to accept that the person takes their criticism seriously. Avoid those easy put-downs or verbal jabs. Responding with "What's your problem?" or "You are one to talk" will not advance the situation. Keep your tone level and your comments constructive—own your part of the interaction. Take the lead and keep it together as it only takes one person to move a discussion from gridlock to connection.

One day I had a good communication laugh with a high-powered journalist. In an overwhelmed teenage rage, her smart, successful, lovely daughter chose to cope in that moment by yelling, "You are a vindictive old woman!" The mother felt attacked but chose a healthy response. She took a moment to pause, relax her jaw, and then responded with, "Hold on there, dear. I may be vindictive, but I am certainly not old! Now keep talking and tell me what is on your mind." A little humor can go a long way. Awesome work by mom.

Bad advice derails good performance, or at least slows it down. When trying to help someone, be clear with your feedback. Make it useful! If the person doesn't get it, try stating it another way and ask for their perspective—and really listen to it. Have a conversation and avoid asserting your authority as no one has all the answers.

Expressing yourself with awareness can so easily calm chaos and engender growth. Getting it right takes self-reflection and some bravery, but good communication promotes performance and fortifies mental health. Avoid the mistrust that defensiveness will cause over time. After all, when trying to help, if you say it right, you can say almost anything.

Chapter Eight

When in Charge of Somebody, Watch It

I had been working with a star NHL player for a few weeks before I met his father. I don't often meet the parents of my adult clients, but this was one invested dad. Carter had always been a leading scorer in the league but had recently fallen way off the pace. He was worried that his season was falling apart so his linemate (one of my clients) gave him my number.

It didn't take Carter and me long to see that his expectations were strangling his execution. Point production was his goal but he hadn't realized that his self-imposed race for points had clouded his focus on the ice. He was overthinking everything. He had been so motivated to achieve a personal best that he got away from his relaxed, consistent game and had stopped doing the things he usually did from shift to shift. He was thinking about how he needed to score rather than how to score.

We had to reduce the unnecessary stress he was creating for himself and readjust his mental approach. After our first meeting he put up six points. After the second, he had four. He obviously had the hang of his new approach and was feeling good. Then the dad showed up.

Carter arrived at our next meeting with his dad and sheepishly asked if he could join us. Thompson seemed keen as he was already headed into my office and had found a seat by the time I caught up. He had been a big influence in Carter's young hockey life as a coach and was a confidant now that Carter was a pro. At thirty years of age, Carter still talked hockey with his father after every game. Knowing this, I assumed that Thompson was excited about Carter's recent results and wanted to be in the meeting to collaborate with us.

When I asked Thompson what he wanted to discuss, he said he didn't have anything, he wanted to observe and hear what I was telling his son. I could see where this was going. I was tempted to kick him out but thought that would make Carter even more uncomfortable than he already was. So I went with it.

What a mistake—one I have never repeated. There sat Thompson, stone-faced and disapproving, while Carter and I did our best to ignore him. Our previous easy give-and-take discussion was nowhere to be seen. The whole thing wasn't working so I ended the session early. At least I got that part right.

Thompson felt threatened when Carter made a change and decided to fix his game without Thompson's customary input. They had been a tight and successful team. By working with me, an outsider, Carter had disrupted their relationship status quo. This momentary shift made the dad feel anxious, like he was losing something, and he wanted to pull his son back within his control. Thompson was thinking of himself and of his rising fear of change between him and his son—he was not thinking about what was helping Carter. Carter never returned to my office.

There was a silver lining, though. Even though Carter didn't continue working with me, he found the courage to change his game on his own despite facing forceful resistance from his father. By the time the dad had reinstated their old roles (by getting Carter out of my office), Carter had already worked through how to keep his focus in check when he felt the pressure of his own expectations. Carter continued his scoring rampage for the rest of the season. That more than worked for me.

Carter's story illustrates just one way parents can interfere with their children's performances, no matter how well meaning they may be. Parents are incredibly powerful. They can be a competitive advantage or feel like a merciless opponent. Most parents want their kids to be happy people and excellent performers. They will provide emotional support, money, time, and more to unlock and develop their child's potential.

Parents can easily optimize the enjoyment and success of their kids of any age by simply doing the basics. Engaging in appropriate behaviors, such as maintaining their composure while watching an event (before and after too), holding on to realistic expectations about their child's abilities, or letting them make or take part in decisions regarding their own situation are all signs of good parenting and mentoring. Emotionally competent, independent people are poised to be able to cope with the stressors of life as well as the pressures of performing.

Too often, parental involvement has proven challenging and demoralizing for all involved. Conflict, hostility, negative attitudes, derogatory comments, controlling behaviors, a hyper focus on results, comparisons to others, or competing with other parents all work against developing a person who can think their way to becoming a great performer, much less a resilient and resourceful person. Whether sport, music, school, or stage, overinvested parents run the risk of putting their kids in an emotional pressure cooker.

The stories in this chapter are about parents and their children in relation to performance, but the lessons here apply to anyone in a position of authority, trust, or power. We can all be supports or mentors and so have a responsibility to understand how to do it well or at least how to not do it badly.

Check your motivations

Parents push, it's part of the job. Being encouraged to step up and take on that daunting but worthwhile opportunity, or to follow through and finish a meaningful task, challenges one to grow and achieve. But some parents don't know the difference between a healthy nudge and a destructive shove.

One mother called me when her daughter was having academic difficulties at university. She wanted to know if I could help Madeline prepare for the stress of her upcoming exams. If she failed again, she would have to leave the institution. I called Madeline but it was too late. Her exams were in days and she knew she was in over her head. She was resigned to do her best but did not pass her program.

When she didn't pass, Madeline was actually relieved to be out from under the pressure of university as she had never wanted to go in the first place. She told her parents she wanted a job in hospitality, not to keep trying to force fit herself into a finance career like they wanted. They wouldn't have it. What would their friends think? *Their* children didn't have jobs; *their* children went to university and had careers like they did. A couple of months later the mother called me and told me she was having Madeline apply to another university. The university in question was even harder to get into than the previous. I was concerned and asked the mother why she would push Madeline to a place where she wouldn't be able to get in, and even if she did (somehow), she wouldn't be able to manage her coursework. It would surely be self-defeating and soul crushing for Madeline. She barely listened. It was clear that her stress over Madeline's success was at the center of the situation.

Curiously, the next I heard was that Madeline did in fact get into this prestigious university. Not so curiously, but shockingly, the mother had set up a scholarship to benefit Madeline's program, essentially buying her daughter's way in. Madeline's mom had knowingly put her daughter in harm's way for her own superficial needs. The enforcement of her parents' ridiculous expectations had compromised Madeline's mental health and she had to seek professional help. She was unable to complete her coursework and never made it to graduation.

Madeline's story is certainly intense, but also emblematic of how parents can lose perspective, which is not uncommon. Many parents don't realize they may be overstepping and would be horrified to think they are. There are those who do too much of their child's homework or push their children's teachers for extra marks and make-up assignments. Some parents heckle referees from the sidelines or overzealously run beside their kids in a cross-country race, shouting at them to dig deeper!

It's not just parents. Others in charge can lose perspective too. Coaches may reward or punish based on perceived effort or personal attitude rather than on merit, just as bosses may promote or ignore based solely on perception or affinity.

When in a position of power, take a step back every now and then. Look at yourself and ensure you are helping your people learn to perform on their own so they can rely on themselves.

We know best

Some parents have stars in their eyes while others have stars in their eyes *plus* access to a naturally talented performer. "We are his parents, we are the only ones who will look out for his best interests," said Shawn and Gemma. There they were, sitting in a fancy private club watching their son, Devon, prepare for his golf event. If Devon did well here, he would earn big prize money and endorsements.

Devon did just that, he won. He quickly stormed the rankings, earning fame for himself. Shawn and Gemma felt powerful. They took control of managing Devon's career. They started shopping for that vacation home they had always talked about. They became increasingly demanding and controlling, mistreating support staff and insisting on daily written reports from trainers on Devon's progress. They did all this while ignoring many of Devon's needs and feelings.

Shawn and Gemma believed they had built a champion from the ground up. After all, they had done everything for Devon his entire life. They took him to tournaments, paid for training, carried bags, made meals, and fought his battles. They rationalized that they had sacrificed for Devon and were owed a return on their investment. They may have thought they were cultivating their son's career, but they ended up looking out for *their* best interests.

Kids are not an investment. Their achievements are for themselves as they are the ones who achieve them. Just because you put time and resources behind getting them to a place of success doesn't mean you will or should get that money back. Helping is part of the job.

It went off the rails, as you might expect. Devon was a great player, but his focus had shifted from trying to play well to *keep winning*. Fun was now fear. He looked for excuses for losing, even for ways to avoid practice. His performance dropped and his happiness too. His parents' initial intention to protect had become destructive.

Few people will ever be in a position to live off their child's success like this, but that same "we know best" sentiment, even in smaller doses, can mar the behavior of even well-intentioned parents.

Get out of the way

Parents still find ways to surprise me. During the MLB draft, I was interviewing a prospective player for one of the teams I consulted with. We were halfway through our video call and I was uncomfortable. The player was evasive and guarded (which wasn't unusual), then would suddenly contradict his responses (which was unusual). Something didn't add up.

He glanced sideways a couple of times as we spoke, so I asked if someone else was in the room. Almost immediately a smiling famous face slid into view. He was the player's father, who also happened to be a Hall of Fame superstar. He had been prompting his son from the shadows—and making a mess of it. He saw himself as the ultimate baseball expert and decided to inject himself into his son's job interview.

He forgot that he was an expert in baseball, not behavioral analytics.

He had made his son appear irrational and impulsive—the kind of player teams don't want to invest in. To the son's relief (and mine), his dad made a quick exit and we were able to finish the interview properly.

When the player was allowed to manage the situation on his own terms, he regained his composure and was able to present his true self. Trusting a person's ability to cope and find solutions to their own life stressors builds self-sufficiency. Use your power as a parent or mentor to generate independence rather than delay it. Sometimes you just have to get out of the way and let things happen. In this case, his father could have spent time helping his son prepare for the interview. He may in fact have had some knowledge to share about what to expect and could have encouraged his son to be relaxed and himself.

Some parents (like any group of people) don't cope well with their emotions. Mimi was trying to pull her daughter out of the junior national championships. Alana was already a tennis champion and her mother was working hard to keep it that way. Alana had won the Under 14 category the previous year (as a thirteen-year-old) and it was time to defend her title. But her mother had other plans.

The tournament schedule had the Under 14s playing at the same time as the Under 16s, so Alana would only be able to play in one tournament. Mimi wanted Alana to play in the Under 16s, but Alana's coaches said no, it was important for her development to play against her own age group again that year. Mimi pressed the coaches, rationalizing that making Alana play girls her own age, whom she had already played and beat, would slow her advance to international stardom. Alana, she argued, must play with older girls who were potentially stronger, faster, and better if she wanted to improve. This time the coaches told Mimi she and Alana could leave the program if she didn't like their decision.

Mimi wouldn't let it go. She came to my office looking for backup. I had worked with Alana since she was twelve. I knew her parents to be involved but this was overkill. I asked Mimi why she was so stressed about something her daughter was clearly capable of doing and her response was that Alana would be very angry if she lost this important tournament to a girl her own age. She went on to say that "if something went wrong and she lost in the final, or didn't even get into the final, I wouldn't know how to help my daughter emotionally."

Of course, this was all nonsense. The previous year, as a younger player in her age category, Alana faced less pressure than the oldest girls and was not expected to win, and so Mimi was relaxed. This year Alana was facing very high expectations to win and Mimi was stressed. And making poor decisions.

For Alana to excel, she needed to be able to control her mental game—Mimi was missing that. Defending her title was a fantastic opportunity to practice managing her emotional control under challenging but appropriate pressure. This was far more beneficial to her future ability to win than "playing up" an age group with no pressure to manage. Being able to win when it matters, or when you really want it, or even when you just think you can win, requires mental ability. It needs to be practiced, not avoided. Mimi was interfering and had become *that* parent: a coach's nightmare. She was getting in Alana's way, inadvertently undermining Alana's future ability to win.

Don't be a Mimi. Caring for your child's future, and wanting the best for their performances, doesn't make you an expert. What a parent can do to help is observe and look for signs of distress (in their child and themselves). In this case, Alana wasn't stressed, her mother was. Parents like to think they know their kids better than anyone, but sometimes they don't, especially when they let their own emotions become the problem. Finding your own emotional discipline will help you better support your child.

Regarding performance in general, having children play up a level (or two) or pushing them for more, whether in sport, school, music, or whatever, can yield benefits—if your child is ready for it and wants it. But too often parents expose their children to unnecessary and unhealthy pressure to enhance their own status. It may be subtle but the "my child is better than yours, so I am better than you" attitude is pervasive.

Relentless pushing will not propel a child to the big time. Developmentally, children will catch up to each other. I am always concerned about the consequences these upgraded performance expectations can take on the mental health of a child or young adult. Physical and emotional maturity are supposed to take time. Let your twelve-year-old play or compete with other twelve-year-olds. Allow them to develop the social and mental skills that will help them perform throughout life. If he or she is better than the rest, it is okay to let them enjoy the ride and the feeling of competence (as it could be fleeting). If they aren't, remember that not all kids want or need to be world-beaters.

Parents who punish

Most parents would agree it's important to support their children, but some parents make that support conditional, which is exceedingly pernicious. Madison's mother, Lindsay, was positive and proud when her daughter won her tennis matches but negative and hurtful when she lost. "When I lose, she freaks out. She starts telling me she won't keep funding me if I don't keep winning and then I won't qualify for tournaments. It is like she thinks I am not trying to win."

Madison found her mother's freak-outs distracting, and it was clear why. "I have learned to end the conversation before she gets crazy, before she tells me I am on my own and that she is done with me."

Madison felt angry and upset every time her mother demeaned her or her efforts. Worse, she had no choice but to endure her mother's inevitable rants.

I called Madison's mom to get her take on the situation and see what we could do. Lindsay was guarded but when she realized our conversation was to help Madison she relaxed. She had been going through some personal stresses herself and welcomed the chance to talk. She had been so drawn into her own difficulties that she didn't realize she was putting so much stress on her daughter. She knew she was hard at times but thought that was how you should motivate someone. We discussed motivation (chapter 5) and how Madison could do it herself if she wasn't so distracted by her mother's harsh judgments.

Because Madison felt she *had* to win, when she didn't she often took her frustrations out on her mother, which in turn upset Lindsay. Madison felt attacked and Lindsay felt unappreciated. It was difficult to decipher how it all started but it didn't matter. They were now in a cycle of defensiveness. They had a monumental discussion, talking about their hurts and hopes and what they appreciated about each other. Lindsay was ready to treat Madison with more respect and Madison was better able to express herself.

It doesn't always go so well. Even the perception of conditional support is damaging over time. Most parents would never think they are making their support conditional because at their core they believe they're doing their utmost to help the children they love. If you want someone to be their best, help them shift *away* from always thinking about results.

As a parent, what you do after a child's performance can be every bit as important as what happens before or during. Brady was quiet. He just wanted to survive the car ride home. Soccer practice was over and it hadn't gone well. He knew what was coming. He got in the car, buckled up, and waited. They hadn't even made it out of the parking lot and his dad's debrief was in motion. "What was that out there? Why didn't you take that shot when you had the chance?" And "It really bothers me when you stand around, it makes you look lazy. You have to work hard all the time, not just some of the time." Brady was going to try to wait it out, but his dad wanted to vent. "You just didn't practice at the level I expect. You have to move your feet and communicate more on the field."

Brady's dad had never played soccer, but he somehow felt obligated to offer precise instructions. The feedback was usually negative and critical, but he always emphasized that he was just trying to make Brady better. Brady wanted to talk to his dad about his play, but this unhelpful criticism was ruining their relationship.

Most parents would be upset to learn that their kids dread the car ride home with them, but that's exactly what can happen when we don't know how to be supportive. Constant criticism becomes just another form of punishment.

Impatience

As we get older it is easy to lose track of how long it can take to mature, to learn how to be an adult. And there is no strict timeline.

One mother brought her high-achieving daughter to see me, frustrated that she was unable to compete at the same skill level she consistently showed in tennis practice. When I sat down with the teenaged Ginny, she told me more. In competition she admitted giving up against players when she thought they were better. As soon as she was losing to a technically stronger player, she would back down mentally. Even if the score was close, her focus would shift to how she couldn't win, which would lead to a string of uncharacteristic errors that would push her further into a negative mindset.

Because she resisted fighting back, she never tested the other player to find out if they were in fact better. She would cruise through the rest of the match on substandard play, feeling righteously resigned. So we worked on it. Her biggest barrier was her tension. When I asked if she knew how to breathe properly to get calm, she laughed and said she held her breath all the time, even when she hit the ball! She learned to breathe with a few easy exercises (chapter 12). Then we had a closer look at her self-talk. She wrote down the negative things she said to herself (out loud for everyone to hear, unfortunately) when games were close. We reworked her self-talk into more constructive strategies that would shift her thoughts back to her game (chapter 14). She decided on one important cue to *do* to execute well (swing through the ball) and wrote it all down in a few bullet points.

Once she knew what to do and was making progress, off she went to play. Eight months later the mother reconnected to let me know that her daughter was doing better than ever but was feeling more anxious than she ever had. The pressure of playing combined with the need to keep up her exceptional grades was causing her to miss sleep. She was "too wound up." It *was* a lot of pressure, and she was only fifteen years old.

I wanted to talk about changing her daughter's schedule for the time being. Why not give her some space and time to regain her equilibrium and perspective? Have her lean on the mental strategies that had already worked so well for her on the court and reapply them to sleep and school and any other pressing concern. What we learn to do to improve performing can apply to the rest of our lives as well. Calm, focused attention, deliberate actions, sticking to a plan in the moment, and reviewing your performances can work wonders on everything from perfecting your serve to getting a good night's sleep. And she was learning these life skills at the right time—when she was young. The mother told me the strategies worked when her daughter used them, but she wouldn't use them enough. Then she added, "I want to talk about medication to lessen her stress."

She felt her daughter was not improving fast enough emotionally, but what fifteen-year-old has the emotional maturity of an adult? The mother was opting for a quick fix rather than a solution that would allow her daughter to learn how to better manage the source of her anxieties. I wanted her daughter to try to learn this control first, then move on to medication only if required.

Medications for anxiety are appropriate when people need them but for situational symptoms and schedule overload like this, learning to take breaks, rest, and cope by using various mental tools is often the best response.

If Ginny got on top of this now, she may be able to move through life's challenges with more tranquility and aplomb. All of us have to learn how to manage stress and anxiety. It can be frustrating to watch a child struggle with these powerful feelings, and the urge to make it better is undeniable. But it is not in anyone's best interests to try to do too much too quickly.

Impatience can take different forms. One father, Harrison, was desperate for his son, Wyatt, to get a university scholarship to the top-ranked rowing program on the East Coast. To secure his offer, Wyatt still had to get his competitive times down and Harrison was relentless in pressuring him to do so. Harrison bought a rowing machine and placed it in the middle of the living room so his son could have all-day access to training. Every day Harrison would point at the rower and ask Wyatt when he was going to sit down and pull a fast time to submit to his prospective coach. All their interactions seemed to revolve around results, more results, and even better results.

Wyatt was becoming so overwhelmed that he began to avoid any attempt at pulling a personal best. He felt he could do it but was too tense to try. High parental pressure was interfering with his performance. Rather than press more, the father needed to take a step back.

So I advised him to. Like many parents, he was surprised as he never considered his role in his son's issue. He thought his son wasn't a natural high achiever like himself and needed a shove to make things happen. In reality, Wyatt had always distinguished himself at school, in the arts and sports. It was the father who was anxious and always in a rush. Harrison's intent was to be supportive, but his constant pestering had become harassing.

It was time to make a deal. I asked Harrison to drop any rowing talk for two weeks so his son and I could talk over his approach to time trials. He agreed and held up his end of the bargain.

When he did get out of the way, Wyatt was able to get the time he needed, and the scholarship. He could have done it sooner and with less drama if the father had detached from the situation earlier and hadn't gone to the trouble of rearranging the living room furniture in the first place.

Performing isn't always easy, for children or parents. So what happens when it gets too tough?

Another teenage client told me through tears that "my dad won't let me quit." Elly was disciplined and dedicated and still couldn't measure up to her own standards in races. She was being surpassed in the pool through no fault of her own and was tired of the embarrassment and failure. Her father insisted that she would just have to work harder. She didn't know how she would endure the remainder of the season and I didn't know what lesson he was trying to impart.

No one is going to oppose persistence in working hard to achieve a goal, but when do you call it? When do you adjust expectations or move on? The answer is, when that goal becomes not only unrealistic but the continued singular dedication to it means that other areas of life are neglected. This is not quitting! This is a healthy shift to a more productive focus.

Goals change, due to many factors, and adjustments need to be made. In this case, Elly's father needed to elevate his daughter's mental well-being by releasing her from his own desires or perhaps vicarious, unfulfilled goals. He was ruining his daughter's joy of the sport along with her self-worth. The emotional damage would be long-lasting.

Of course, not all parents ride their children this hard, but it is common to advise kids to "never quit." This can often be the wrong advice. Rather than seeing it as quitting, think about it as making some room for them to pursue their next positive adventure in life.

Where are the good parents?

They are everywhere! But you might not notice them because they are doing their jobs well. To be a good performance parent you only need to cover the basics.

Supportive parents keep their composure during events and require the same from their performer. They stay positive or at least neutral when watching. They reinforce the importance of being a "good sport" (no matter what age their "sport" is). And they listen to those who work with their kids.

Good parents let coaches coach, even if those parents actually do have expert knowledge and experience. They realize that coaching from the sidelines is emotionally driven and disruptive to group cohesion. They include their children (even young ones) in decisions that pertain to them and don't make their relationship all about performance results, good or bad. They ask their children's opinions and hold realistic expectations.

No one is perfect. Good performance parents understand what stresses them while watching their children and find ways to cope. If you get anxious and find it difficult to watch your performer compete, it may be best to stay home. Or if watching with your partner frustrates you, sit elsewhere. Brady's dad figured it out. He decided to stop going to every one of his son's soccer practices. When he did go, on the way home he was purposeful in his communication. He would tell himself to "stay quiet, and start with something positive." He asked Brady more questions and listened to his answers. Brady started to like his dad's company again.

It's important to recognize what stresses your kids, too, and help them cope. One of the simplest and most effective things you can do is give them a safe place to complain and work out their worries. It's tempting to interfere, to try to do more to help, but we can't protect a child from losing.

Maybe your performer does need to toughen up. I watched as a parent reamed her teenage son out after a competitive karting race because she felt he quit when things weren't going his way. She was angry at his attitude and that he would be such a poor sport. If he was going to behave this way then he was wasting his time and hers for coming to watch. Sounds harsh, but I thought she had it right. Her motivations were good: she just wanted her son to try his best, win or lose, and so this was an occasion where a shove was warranted. It took a few minutes, but her son realized she had it right too. She didn't care if he came dead last, she cared that he put his best foot forward.

Good parenting and mentoring means engaging in the discussion with your performer as you won't always have the answers. It means promoting autonomy and self-reliance, having them do things for themselves so they can move through life with an ability to cope with adversity and take action. What does that look like? It can be as simple as letting children do their own university applications and helping only if they come to you for assistance. Or commenting positively on their effort and not just their grades.

Some parents are never satisfied. If their child loses, the parents get angry; if they win, it goes uncelebrated and underappreciated because winning is expected. Your authority can create stress and strain or promote feelings of competence and positive mental well-being. As a parent you're not just helping them succeed now, you're helping them learn to overcome the inevitable setbacks they will face, and perform at their best, for the rest of their lives, no matter what they do.

Chapter Nine

Why Character Counts

S port franchises and companies often ask my opinion on an athlete or candidate before they commit to signing a contract. Sometimes I sit in on interviews and observe, but most times I'm asked to interview someone directly. I'm not interested in how high they can jump or past successes. I'm looking at other qualities.

I was conducting these one-on-one interviews for an NFL team, assessing if new players would be an asset or potentially a liability. Before one interview, the director of pro scouting popped his head into the room and casually said, "Hey Dana, when you interview this next guy, make sure you leave the door open a little." He must have expected the confused look on my face, as he readily added, "This player has a few 'incidents' on his record and is kind of unpredictable, so a couple of us will be out here in the hall in case he gets aggressive."

WAIT, WHAT?! I reflexively scooted my chair back to put more space between me and where the player would be sitting and moved my pen into "jabbing" position (like I was in a parking garage, alone, at night). What was I thinking? If a three-hundred-pound athlete decided to lose his cool, I'd have no chance of protecting myself (pointy pen at the ready or not).

The NFL draft process is always intense as a poor selection can set a franchise back financially, on the field, and with fans, but this was a new wrinkle for me. I'll often get negative comments and hostile attitudes from talent evaluators when I provide a contrary take on a talented prospect that they covet. But I had never had to consider the possibility of actually getting punched out. Which begs the question, in my mind anyway, why would you consider drafting a player if you knew his behavior was unpredictable or problematic on and off the field?

The team's draft notes on this player indicated that he had "anger issues" and "consistent character issues." Yet, the front office seemed to think they could somehow channel this person's impulsive outbursts into a controlled ferocity for use on the field. This prospect was clearly a red flag, yet the decision-makers were seriously considering bringing him into their organization. They were underestimating the impact character can have on talent, potential, and performance.

Think of character as a measure of a person's ability to act in a self-disciplined, considerate, and appropriately restrained manner. Does the individual think through their actions? Can they see another person's point of view? Do they behave appropriately in a variety of situations? Character is the horsepower driving their daily decisions and actions. While some people are naturally better at behaving rationally and responsibly, others are natural disasters waiting to happen.

When I help teams draft players or organizations hire employees, part of my job is to look for potential. I highlight those candidates or prospects who are better able to perform with success on a consistent basis. Remember NHL player Cole in chapter 1? His constellation of natural characteristics spurred him to improve his performance over time, vastly improving his game beyond what the scouts predicted. I will flag other people, like the high NHL draft pick Benny, so I can indicate to the organization the specific behaviors this person will need to manage to be able to hit their potential or hit it faster.

The other part of my job is to identify who is more likely to fail, despite how talented they may be. I red-flag these people as they are at another level of conduct altogether. They are extreme in their behavior and find it very difficult to change. It may be disquieting, but not everyone can be successfully developed or miraculously mentored.

I assign a red flag to those players or employees who will consistently fail to control their emotions under pressure, either in their professional or personal lives. Due to their talent, this lack of self-regulation is often rationalized and tolerated by management. A person who is toxic in terms of low impulse control, lack of self-discipline, questionable conscious restraint, or an unwillingness to see others' points of view can easily destroy an organization's performance culture, which takes years to develop. Don't be fooled by a red flag's periodic bouts of good behavior, as these individuals are rarely able to change, grow, or progress in meaningful ways.

Spotting red flags

What do red flags look like? Mason is a good example.

During an NBA team's internal draft talks, personnel from management, scouting, medical, and sport science were all asked to weigh in on the team's top prospects. All was going smoothly until it was my turn to present on Mason. My general comments included: he tends to be inconsistent on the floor; he will openly clash with the coaching staff if he disagrees with their decisions; he is self-oriented, so more interested in his own needs and loves the spotlight; he will be difficult to manage on and off the floor over a long season. I looked up and saw nothing but blank stares all around the room.

Nobody wanted to hear that Mason was a red flag. One scout countered, "But he doesn't play that way. Sure, he can be fiery, but he is as tough as they come." He had spent months watching this player and he didn't want any "attitude crap" undermining his hard work. He saw potential and talent and that was that.

"He can certainly be tough," I agreed, "but you won't see that from him every game. In fact, he will have trouble playing hard for a full game. He is moody and his energy will be up and down. He is short-tempered and has a tendency to snap when he gets frustrated."

Another scout agreed with me, saying he'd seen that behavior in the player too. But I wasn't done, there was more: "He often won't take the time to think through consequences before he acts, and is unreliable, on and off the floor. I don't think he will be able to rein himself in on demand."

The organization did not draft Mason, but over the next five years they traded for him and traded him away, *twice*. Both stints ended due to his behavior: inconsistent play, an unwillingness to listen to the directives of the head coach, and bad behavior away from the game, too. Character counts.

It can be hard to see red flag behaviors at first glance but eventually they will emerge. Jay was the CEO of a PR firm. He had been at the top for more than a decade. But working for Jay was difficult. He fiddled with the accounting, fudged his credentials, exaggerated his contributions, and blamed others for his mistakes. He was a big talker and would say whatever he wanted to get himself into or out of a situation. He promised projects and promotions but failed to follow through. Jay was in his position not because he had been a sought-after candidate but because he kept ahead of his transgressions. He would move to another firm before his behavior was exposed. Jay never changed, but he always left a wake of distress behind him. If only his current employer had done more to learn about his past work before bringing him on board.

If your character is more mature, you think through your actions and behave appropriately most of the time, even under stress and pressure. But red flags continually act in ways that bring down others, affect organizational culture, and eventually harm everyone's performance (even if they seem to boost overall success at first).

Red flags and organizational culture

Jeremy had finally done it. It took him two years, but he had unified the baseball clubhouse against him. Half the players wanted him out and the other half did their best to ignore him. He was clearly a superior athlete, both physically and technically, and was supposed to be on his way to stardom. If only he could control his destructive impulses.

When things were going his way, he was loud, undisciplined, and selfish. When they weren't, he was loud, undisciplined, and selfish. Sure, he could be fun and charming, but he also yelled and picked fights. He threatened a teammate with a bat. He was frequently late and broke clubhouse rules. Sometimes he practiced with intent, other times he just goofed around and chatted. He partied often and had a hard time calling it a night in time to get some sleep. He got the kind of speeding tickets that could get your license suspended. You never knew what mood you would find him in. It was unintentional but he was toxic. Jeremy just couldn't seem to help himself.

Even the coaching staff had given up on him, but the front office kept searching for ways to make him play better and fit in with at least some of his teammates. Nothing was working but they couldn't admit defeat. After all, he was capable of good behavior, sometimes. They had fallen in love with their own visions of Jeremy's potential. They thought they had scooped the entire league by signing a "generational player" that other teams had somehow missed. Initially they were smug and self-congratulatory but were now aggravated with Jeremy's lack of production, his antics in the clubhouse, and his bad behavior away from the stadium. The big money he was paid, the mentors, the security detail that followed him around in an attempt to keep him out of trouble, the heart-to-heart talks with the owner and general manager, all the babysitting was not moving the needle on this guy. Jeremy's character was stifling his performance and fracturing the team culture. He was looking more and more like a total bust.

Finally, the front office stopped holding out hope. They realized they had rationalized and accepted his behavior for too long. They acknowledged the serious harm of their poor investment and traded him.

But it was too late. Jeremy's protracted presence in the organization had damaged the dynamic of the team on the field and in the clubhouse. Team rules were enforced for some but not others. Players complained and staff became negative. Entitlement and mistrust created different groups and agendas. Not everybody was driven to win, some didn't care anymore. Morale had eroded and the executive leadership was being questioned. Character can transcend the individual. It can enhance or diminish the performance culture of your team. When you realize you have a red flag, don't hang on, move them out before they cost you too much.

We have a red flag, now what?

Knowing to look for red flags is the first step. Identifying them is the second. Once you've spotted one, what can you do about it?

In the off-season, a team asked me to interview a potential acquisition, Lucas. They had a shot at signing an exceptional yet controversial player. Apparently, the word around the league was that Lucas had "too much personality." He had a history of disciplinary action and demotions, but the team still felt he was worth a look. I agreed, as it is always best to get an accurate accounting of who the person is, of what happened and why, and talking to the individual is a big part of the puzzle. Unfortunately, reputations can be marred by exaggerations or lies, whether purposeful or inadvertent. I have seen many situations where employers, staff, or colleagues make life unnecessarily difficult for some people, whether for self-gain, self-protection, or some other motive. After all, poor character doesn't skip over those in power.

After watching Lucas impress the coaches during his on-field workout, we met at the hotel for our interview. I enjoyed his engaging energy and easy positivity, but Lucas couldn't help flying his red flag a little too high. His low impulse control fueled his tendency to say whatever he wanted whether it was true or not, and regardless of who it hurt. He acted on emotion without making a conscious effort to think through his actions. He thought he was just fun-loving and at times he was, but he took it too far too often. It was all about him. His immature and self-ruinous behavior had been unabating throughout his career and his lack of discipline made redemption look out of reach, at least for the short term.

Incredibly, the team still wanted to offer him a contract, and a substantial one at that. I felt this was a high-risk move that would require extra support and care for Lucas, as well as an exit plan for the team. The owner and general manager agreed. We would provide Lucas with the resources that would best promote his well-being and allow him to make the most of himself and his game. The accompanying caveat was that at the first sign of bad behavior, the team would seek to trade Lucas in an effort to protect the organization financially and from the inevitable fan base outrage. Lucas and his agent agreed.

Training camp went well, and Lucas's contribution looked promising, but within weeks he was back to his true self. Veteran players and personnel took exception to his low standards and self-serving attitude. He was continually unprepared for practice and criticized teammates and coaches for his own mistakes. The season hadn't even started and management saw what was coming. They moved swiftly and traded him three days later.

If you see a red flag, seriously consider if your organization can manage the possible costs to your performance culture and/or your productivity. If you want to proceed anyway, have an exit strategy. And make clear boundaries for yourself and the person in question so they know what is coming if they cross your line. Some behaviors are extremely difficult to change over the long term. And some people who exhibit them won't put in the effort to change. So, all you can do if you have a red flag is hope for the best and support that outcome. Do everything and anything you can to help that person, but plan for the worst.

Less talent, more character

Building a successful business or team is a lot easier when you have the right people. Those who can add significantly to the performance of your group are key ingredients to quality results. Interestingly, avoiding a red flag may be even more important than finding people with skill and talent.

While many people mature with experience and age, red flags tend to struggle more in their approach to life. These individuals are much more likely to behave in thoughtless, inconsiderate ways. They are generally self-serving, can act impulsively, or disregard rules for their own satisfaction. They are emotional and ready to complain. They tend to tolerate lower standards for themselves and others, enjoy rebelling, and avoid being socially responsible. They *can* try to make a conscious effort to think through their actions or try to avoid doing things just for their own gain, but such efforts are not reliable over the long haul.

A senior publishing executive told me about his "character rule" when signing potential authors to book deals. He had just met with a high-profile business leader who would surely land on the bestseller list. The problem was that the publisher left the meeting feeling strongly that this corporate boss would be his usual arrogant and condescending self when working alongside the publisher's high-level team of editors and public relations and marketing specialists. Even though this future author was only, say, half a red flag, the publisher was unwilling to expose his people to morale-busting treatment.

Tough decisions like that take courage and integrity. If you can avoid difficult people in the selection process, you should do so, as no amount of sensitivity training is going to change the core of a red flag individual. If you recognize a red flag in your organization and see that they are disrupting your group unnecessarily, strongly consider terminating them. Let them go with care of course, but sooner rather than later.

Many businesses fail to be accountable for their red flags. It is easier to ignore them and hope for the best, especially if you are excited by the opportunity to bring in a rainmaker or a super talent. But red flags put an organization's long-term viability at risk. No organization can absorb a red flag without consequence. Those that do it better have exercised strong leadership and a willingness to discipline those who step beyond the organization's core vision and values. Even so, they eventually lose good people or gain a reputation as a problematic or noxious place to work.

It's not so difficult to avoid a bad situation if you do your due diligence up front. When hiring, check the candidate's references, and ask specifically about character and personality. Investigate: Were there any issues? Any confrontations of note? I say "of note" because, let's face it, some confrontations are appropriate and necessary. For instance, if you feel there has been a mistake in your performance review or something is being said about you that isn't true, why wouldn't you confront the situation to make it right? Confrontation doesn't have to be contentious.

Working for the right people is important too. In my consulting practice, I have learned the hard way to look for red flags before I join an organization. I once signed a contract with a professional sports team and was weeks into the season when the front office called me upstairs for a meeting. This was the second time that management sat me down and pressured me to provide them with a daily list of the names of the players I was talking to as well as notes on what we were talking about. Of course I said no, again. So they fired me. I was upset about the whole mess, but it worked out well as clearly that wasn't the place for me. Breaking client confidentiality is obviously never an option and they knew it. They just didn't care. It was a bad fit and I didn't catch on to that beforehand because I assumed they would do the right thing by their players. Now I make sure.

An NBA owner once called me in a panic while in the middle of a stressful player contract negotiation. He immediately blurted out, "You don't think he will hurt me, do you?" He was actually scared for his physical safety. Nobody needs that. If you are going to purposefully invite a red flag into your organization (not recommended), make sure you can move that person out with minimal damage or loss. If you end up working for a red flag, purposefully (also not recommended) or not, be prepared to cut ties, hopefully with minimal upset or loss. If a person is difficult in the extreme and likely to upend your team, is their skill set worth the cost to employee well-being, productivity, or to your broader performance culture? My experience says it is not.

Your performance culture is worth protecting. Groups that do it right are willing to avoid or eliminate red flags. This takes foresight and control as it can be very enticing to hire a big talent despite knowing there could be big consequences. Good cultures minimize these potential derailers. They always look for new talent but also focus on getting the most out of the talent they already have.

Good cultures decide where they are going. They have clear goals and defined roles for everyone. They deal in individuals, by which I mean organizations tend to get their best results when each person is emboldened to do *their* best. They have reasonable rules with follow-through—people know where the line is and what is expected.

They talk too. Good performance cultures are positive and straightforward. They challenge underperformers and help them improve rather than ignore them and expect the high performers to take on more to pick up the slack. There are exchanges and conversations. Some are intense and demanding but there is listening and expressing of the good and the bad. Individuals hear about what they are doing well and are encouraged with specific technical or mental coaching to work out how to do the other things better. There is kindness and respect too.

Communication won't help much with red flags, but it makes a monumental difference to your performance culture when you have strong character to work with. Good cultures actively promote individual accomplishment not just because it promotes team results but because it is the right thing to do.

Invest in character. Its power is underestimated.

Part Two

How to Perform Under Pressure

Chapter Ten

Shift When You Drift!

Leaving your performance to chance is, well, chancy. The day before an important match on the world tour, a professional squash player mentioned to me that he was "a bit nervous, as I don't feel like I've fully found my shots, so I am hoping that tomorrow I'll just relax and play." This client was ranked highly in the world and knew exactly how to hit his shots! He was giving up. He didn't want to lose, but he was letting this fear distract him from his game.

Letting "hope" dictate his play, instead of his own actions on the court, was nonsense. The solution? "How about shifting your thinking onto something concrete and reliable like the plan we talked about? If you stick to that, you will do the best you can, which will make you happy. If you decide to wing it, who knows how you will play?" He shook his head slowly like he was fed up with himself (or me) and said, "I really want to win, but I am being a baby, aren't I? I know I need to shut up about my worries and shift my focus back onto what I am going to do on court." Yup, exactly. It's excellent advice for all of us: performing great doesn't just happen, you make it happen, for yourself.

How you perform under pressure is predictable. If you can stay calm and focused enough, you will have a good day. If you get too tense and your focus drifts, your performance will cave in on you. Even if your emotions feel random or destructive when you face pressure, they don't have to be; you can nudge them back into place. You really can.

It is critical to have a framework or a process to help you navigate through your pressures. The most important skill for a performer to develop is to be process oriented, not results driven. Results are a consequence of what you do, while a process guides you through what to do. That is why over time I have put together a process that clients find clear and powerful for staying focused on the actions they need to achieve the results they are aiming for. Every client learns to use this framework to their benefit, no matter their job or performance situation.

Before you can begin to establish your new mental approach to pressure, think about how your performances typically unfold. I like to organize the patterns of performing into good days and not-so-good days. For instance, when it comes to performing, everybody knows what a good day is like. You feel calm and confident, you automatically stay focused on execution, your assignments, your script, the topic, the steps of a procedure, or the answer to a question. You are not even aware of thinking at all (you are thinking, it is just that you are attending to effective thoughts!), and most salient, you are not worrying about what the result will be or how you will do. You are drawn into the task and connected to what it takes to accomplish it properly. You perform effortlessly—your emotional chemistry is simply there with no need for mental adjustments. You're in control, doing your thing!

But these quality performance days can be frustratingly elusive. Some days, often for no apparent reason, you feel distracted, tense, or fully immersed in *how* you are doing rather than paying attention to *what* you are doing. You may be thinking too much or thinking about the wrong things like results or your own expectations. You fuss about what other people may be thinking about you, worry about making a mistake, feel low in confidence, or fear that you will fail. On these bad days you are distracted from the task and your performance breaks down.

The mental shift from good to not-so-good, or to outright bad, can be stunningly quick. It can happen from one day to the next, in the middle of a game or event, or even move back and forth within the same task. These are the tough days. These mental disruptions are what we need to prepare for.

Sometimes you start well and then drift. I was in Italy watching my beach volleyball team compete in an Olympic qualifying event and was really enjoying the high-level action. My team had just won the first set against the top team in the world. They were playing their game; they were technically sharp and moving with easy energy. During the break between sets I could see that they were communicating with each other and looked relaxed and ready.

But as soon as the second set started, I saw it: The drift was on. Their first few serves went into the net or out of the court. Their passing was off, and they had trouble finishing points. They had played the entire first set in the "good day" mental box and somehow got slammed into the "bad day" box within the first few minutes of the second set. Why it happened doesn't matter; what matters is what happened next.

We had prepared a plan specifically for this, what to do when they started to beat this higher-ranked team. But they didn't shift. All I could do was watch as they quickly lost the second set.

Why would we prepare a plan for when we're winning? Even though they knew what to do, they tensed up, rather than keeping their focus on technique. This is common for everyone! They let their thoughts shift to the "what ifs," the possible mistakes, and the fact that they could finally beat this team and secure their spot for the Olympics. Their thinking had shifted from trying to win to trying not to lose, and they were in trouble.

Going into the deciding third set, they began to show signs of re-membering their plan. They slowed down between points. I could see them breathing properly, exhaling while setting up to serve and con-tacting the ball with their whole hand, not just part of their hand. On defense they showed patience and waited to see where the ball was going before they moved rather than trying to guess and moving too soon.

This last set was back-and-forth but my team won because they slowed down enough to be able to shift their thinking. One player actually yelled at her partner to "just get the f-cking ball in the court!" when she went to serve. It was a timely reminder for the partner to stop drifting and zone in on her target on the other side of the net rather than trying to muscle the ball over the net.

I don't necessarily recommend yelling and cursing at someone, but sometimes you have to be ready to snap yourself or someone else to attention. In pressure moments we may need to be momentarily sharp with ourselves or others just to stop the flow of noise in our heads. The reminder to "shut up and shift" is a useful way to momentarily break your connection with any mental jumble so you can quickly shift to a better focus point. This team had a plan (so they knew certain comments would be coming from a place of love) and they shifted to it just in time to win a hard-fought match. Never overlook the fact that playing well can be just as distracting as playing poorly!

This team knew what to do and were prepared, but still lost their focus for a while. For others, bad days can happen when you think you are ready but you're not. Later that day, back at my hotel, I watched another mind drift and shift, this time at a Grand Slam tennis tournament happening elsewhere in the world. My player had expected to win his match against a lower-ranked player. Rolling through an opponent in straight sets would be a welcome start (mentally and physically) to the tournament. The first set was an easy win—for the other guy. From the start my player was under stress and on his heels. His errors were unforced and his temper flared. He was now thinking about how terrible he would feel if he lost to this "lousy player" and got bounced from the tournament early. He needed to shift.

During the changeover before the next set, I could see him pulling his focus back to the plan we had discussed on the phone earlier in the day. He sat quietly, leaned back in his seat, and took some controlled slow breaths. His angry emoji face melted into a loose, relaxed one. He was clearly doing a good job reconnecting to what he had to do on the court. He controlled the next three sets and won the match.

He hadn't underestimated his opponent's skill level; he had overestimated his own mindset. Against this player he had assumed his mind would stay put, but he got ahead of himself and was thinking about future matches and potential glory. I want people to dream about wonderful triumphs and consider improvements to make, but not during a match. His focus wasn't there from the start, and it derailed his play. To his great credit, he showed excellent presence by recognizing his mistake, and then shifting back to his mental plan and back to his game.

Be ready from the start, check in on yourself. Whether you are feeling good or not, we all need to have a plan ready and remind ourselves in the moment to connect to it. You have to be ready to shift when you inevitably drift. Don't leave it to chance.

Results are important for any performance, but you must not linger in that mind space. Yes, you need to know the score, when to pick up the pace in the operating room, a race, or an exam, when to stop talking in an interview or during a conflict. You need to know how you are doing. But your job is to pluck out this critical, evaluative information and then quickly shift back to the task. And keep on shifting when you need to because one shift is usually not enough. Does the process always work? It does when you use it! Will it always make you win? No, of course not, but it will take you to your best on that day. It may take some practice and determination, but yes, it works.

The Process

Recognizing the need to shift is the starting point. You have to have a plan for how you'll do it, and that plan has to be customized for you. Effective plans are simple plans, and I've found the best process to organize your mental approach has three steps.

Step 1:   First, in the next chapter you will list your hot spots, or those distractions that worry or bother you before or during a performance. This list will enable you to spot your own super derailers, the ones you need to combat the most.

Step 2:   Next, you will dip into the four mental skills that best control performance, chapters 12–15, one for each skill. You can use all the skills, and subsequent strategies, before and during an event, or only one. Just use something!

Step 3:   Lastly, you will choose your favorite strategies and organize them into a go-to solution that you can reference to help you shift in the moment. Ultimately, your plan will be so simplified that it can fit on a Post-it Note!

All plans look different because every performer and performance scenario is unique. But when they're done right, all plans accomplish the same thing. In the following chapters we'll look at five real-life performers as they move through their concerns and frustrations to reveal their go-to plan, the one they follow in the moment. Each performer deals with a different concern, and all use these three steps to formulate a new, effective approach to their performance situation. As you read, think about your own performance wants or needs. You'll be able to use the same tools and process to customize your own plans. You can use the Fun Homework at the back of this book as a guide for keeping track of your ideas and solutions, or keep a journal, or use your phone—whatever is best for you.

Our performers cover a range of challenges. Riley is forced to confront his lack of confidence while playing in the NHL. Cameron's desire to be perfect interferes with her ability in social situations at work. As an NFL quarterback, Ty realizes that avoiding conflict with his coach is not doing him any favors. Alex, a world-ranked top tennis prospect, works through her constant worry about what other people are thinking, especially her opponents. And Jamie wrangles with his emotional outbursts, the kind that he always regrets. Each will move their performance from bad to better, discouraging to satisfactory, unremarkable to remarkable, or stellar to inspired. And so can you.

Chapter Eleven

Hot Spots:
Figure Out What Messes You Up

We know that some people are naturally better at certain things than others. Some people crave any opportunity to get up in front of a crowd and prattle on, while others are tortured at the thought of having to speak up in class to get that 25 percent participation mark. What is easy for one person may be very difficult for another. How do you get better? How do you minimize a weakness or learn to act rather than react? The first step is to figure out what gets in your way and makes you falter.

Everybody I work with wants to be better at something. It could be to stop taking "stupid penalties" during a hockey game, to act less awkward (or more relaxed) in social settings, to more effectively deal with a critical person (be it a coach, boss, or parent)—even getting a blood test despite hating needles. These performance situations can be any event in which you need or want to excel but for whatever reasons end up holding back in the moment.

People hold back because they become distracted by results, fears, expectations, glory, or other pressures (real or imagined) and behaviors (their own or others'). Distractions are those psychological barriers that can get between you and your best. They frustrate, puzzle, scare, or just really bug you. Not all are equal and some, if left unattended, will derail your performance, so it's important to separate those that are simply a bother from those that do damage.

What do derailing distractions look like? I heard a great example on, of all places, my flight back from working at the Indianapolis 500. My very interesting seatmate and I recognized each other from a talk I had given to her surgical residency group. She told me about her biggest distraction, her super derailer. After my presentation at her hospital, she had taken a moment to write a list of the distractions that had the potential to disrupt her best surgical work. She mentioned things like having an inexperienced assistant or annoyance over scissors that do not cut well (I guess so!). But her primary hot spot, she realized, was being observed by the attending surgeon, who is the big boss in the operating room. When she was being evaluated, she tensed up before she even picked up a scalpel. Who wouldn't be tense when learning to repair someone's aorta or carotid artery? Now add to that a figure of authority observing you, and a patient expecting you to be flawless.

In this overly primed state, flooded with feelings of being judged and thoughts of underperforming, she would rush through her equipment setup. She explained that as a petite person she needed an extra minute or two to optimize her operating environment. She always had to adjust the position of everything from tables and stools to lights and instruments. Under the watchful gaze of an experienced surgical team ready to begin, those minutes felt like forever! To release the pressure to keep the pace, she unwittingly slipped into "express" setup mode, which interfered with her comfort and skill level during the entire evaluation. Having taken the time to think through a distraction that was significant to her, she became aware that she had to make an adjustment in her setup preparation, even if the attending surgeon seemed impatient. Optimizing her setup environment took the edge off her tension and left her ready to focus on good operating, garnering outcomes commensurate with her outsize talent.

Determining your hot spots is not a difficult task. People are often very aware of the things that diminish their performance, but they may hide from them or hope they will go away on their own. If you can't say what is in the way (even to yourself), you won't learn how to get around it. As the saying goes, if you keep doing what you are doing, you will keep getting what you are getting. So, I ask my clients outright, "What's up? What is bothering you?" Typically, they tell me. They know what annoys and frustrates them and what situations they dread, and want a solution, which is what they came for in the first place.

For others who may be unsure, too upset to focus, or less aware, the conversation may be longer, but the worries and barriers still rise to the surface. One of my NFL clients called me and announced that he was "in the dumps" and wanted to talk. I had first worked with him when I was consulting for the team that drafted him. Since then, he had been enjoying a great career elsewhere and had multiple Super Bowl rings to show for it. After catching up on each other's news we got right to it, and I asked what was messing him up. He said he wasn't sure, but that he was feeling overwhelmed and sorry for himself. His emotions had become entangled and if we were going to get anywhere, we had to drill down and get to the specifics of his discomfort.

I asked general questions about his work and home life, as well as what was going well and what wasn't. We both listened as he rid himself of his frustrations. It turns out that he was playing with an injury (again), had contract issues to deal with in the off-season, was busy (happily, but still busy!) with a little daughter and a pregnant wife, had his house broken into, and was not even starting in games. He was tired, sore, and felt ripped off.

By venting, he was able to unload his distress and see his distractions more clearly: having to perform at the highest level when he was not 100 percent healthy; concern about his future; perceiving not starting in games as a lack of respect from his coach; and at this moment, diminishing confidence. Then he said, "I need to play better." He had a list of legitimate stressors, but he had zeroed in on what was really bothering him.

"Are you able to play better or are you at your limit?" I wanted to know that he was being objective relative to his injury and his talent. I feel there is no sense in erroneously expecting too much from yourself; it is better to know your upper limits and perform great within them. "I can play better," he said. "I am doing my job, I guess, but I am not making the big, impactful plays that I should be. I am scared that my season is going downhill, which has been in my head and holding me back on the field."

He had it. Step 1 complete. He was on his way out of the dumps. Listing all his distractions allowed him to isolate what was actually derailing his performance. When he wasn't making big plays he drifted mentally and his overall game suffered. He had found his super derailer and we could now strategize around it.

For those who are less forthcoming or prefer to look away from themselves, a checklist is handy. I sometimes offer a list of distractions to people to get the ideas rolling. I find it's also helpful for people to see they are not alone—the checklist is made of common distractions that lots of people face and it helps them acknowledge what is on their mind. As they check off what distractions apply to them, they feel more comfortable and add more of their own.

When you are serious about exploring your hot spots, you may have to sit with some discomfort. Perhaps you drive your spouse to despair because you are perpetually late. You know you are always pushing punctuality, but you avoid taking ownership. You blame external excuses beyond your control, like traffic or weather or that you had one last thing to do. Gather your courage and ask yourself, "Am I being honest with myself?" Take a moment to make sure you don't automatically deflect or defend, because if you do, you may have located a hot spot worth tweaking.

One Major League Baseball player I worked with preferred to blame the umpire when he struck out. He would mutter and pout his way back to the dugout, but lately would also walk over to the bat rack and take a swing (or two) at it, sending splinters flying everywhere. We chatted about it during batting practice one day. He was embarrassed about failing at the plate, not about his tantrums. Ultimately, he had to admit that self-criticism was the disrupting force, it was his current super derailer. From there, he could move on to learning how to stay focused at bat. If you "lose it" in response to some unmet need or desire, you have probably nailed a hot spot that messes you up.

When you first write your list, it can look overwhelming. Do not worry! This is expected. Your list could have twenty or more items, but you will only have to plan for the few that hurt the most. If you deal with these big ones, the others fade into the background as they were never the issue in the first place. Review your list carefully and skip over those items that don't cause much angst, ticking off the ones that do—these are your super derailers.

Distractions are plentiful and always close by. Some are fleeting and meaningless while others are intrusive and damaging. Know the difference and be ready to handle the ones that matter. But first, let's look at the specific distractions that our real-life performers are up against.

Riley the NHL Player:
"I am not playing with confidence"

Riley's playing time was diminishing quickly because he wasn't playing as well as he practiced. He didn't understand why he was playing poorly or know what to do about it. When we sat in a hotel lobby to find a solution, he was dejected and said he had no confidence in his game. "I feel like I am a naturally gifted athlete but lack the mindset in some moments. When I am hot I am really confident, but when I'm not playing well I get inside my own head and make it worse on myself."

Riley was clearly a player who could contribute but was anxious and concerned that he couldn't or wouldn't. In this situation it is always best to start by looking at the "now." I asked him to think about his recent practices and games and tell me what he typically did on the ice. He said in practice he was dynamic. He was fast and used his speed to take the puck to the net, and he backchecked hard. During games he found himself standing around, squeezing his stick too hard, hoping not to get the puck so he wouldn't make a mistake. I asked him what he was thinking about during games, and what situations made him tense, and it didn't take long for him to list his distractions:

*   I worry about results, my personal stats, and if I will get any points.

*   I think about how much time I will get on the ice.

*   I wonder what line I will be on, or if I'll get moved down a line, or if I will even get to dress for the game (this really messes with my confidence).

*   If we are playing at a "bad rink" (in an arena where I have had a bad game in the past) I am a little nervous that I will have a bad game.

*   When I overanalyze my play during the game (while on the bench between shifts, grabbing the iPad and watching my shifts).

*   When I feel too self-critical and doubt myself even though I am a good player.

*   When I rush during my shift, as in dumping the puck into the corner when I should hold on to it and make a play.

*   When I feel like I must play well for my dad and friends.

*   Any negative self-talk like, "What are you doing?"

*   When someone "chirps" (trash-talks) me I get frustrated and then I start talking at the referees instead of playing my game.

*   Thinking about a lousy shift earlier in the game or worrying what the coach is thinking of my play can also unsettle me.

*   Not sleeping great, especially during the season.

While any of these items could be distracting, only a few were likely to derail his performance. The next step was to separate super derailers, those distractions that went beyond typical mental noise to cause trouble. Riley reviewed his list and highlighted the top three obstacles he felt had a destructive impact on his play: worrying about results and personal stats like putting up points, thinking about how much time he will get on the ice or if he'll even be in the lineup, and thinking about what his dad or coach is going to say about any mistakes.

Riley realized that when he is thinking about these, his performance will break down. He knew he couldn't possibly be focused on skating with the puck and making smart plays if he was worrying about making a mistake and whether the coach will sit him for the remainder of the period. Knowing his super derailers allowed us to move on to the next step, determining the strategies that he could shift onto to keep him focused on his game.

Cameron the New Leader:
"This needs to be perfect"

When it comes to performing, it is time to forget perfect. Excessive self-recriminations and attempts to appear flawless are scripts for self-defeat. The only likely outcome of requiring perfection from yourself is failure, and failure sparks unpleasant reactions such as unhealthy self-blame, self-criticism, and guilt.

Cameron's recent promotion to a leadership position at a top private school required more engagement in social and networking events. Now, in addition to teaching, she would be hosting alumni events, asking people for money at fundraising dinners, and having difficult conversations with parents. All the social situations that made her feel uncertain and anxious. Why? Because these settings were new and unfamiliar to her. In the classroom, she was experienced, she was excellent, and she was in control. She loved the structure that teaching provided as she could plan meticulously and overprepare for the day thereby avoiding mistakes and ensuring a "perfect" outcome. This was her safe zone. Also, as a quiet, shy person she was more comfortable with people one at a time or small groups of people she knew. With her new responsibilities she would have to interact with large groups of people she didn't know in more free-flowing social settings.

She was a minimum risk-taker and liked high odds before proceeding. Now she was stepping into the spotlight without a script. She could feel inner pressure to project an image of easy competence, not rattled awkwardness. How could she be accepted and respected if she appeared inadequate or inferior? Cameron's distraction list included:

* Focusing on results, specifically asking, "Will I do a good job? Do I have what it takes? Do I trust my capacity to deliver on this next step in my career? Am I a fraud, do I have imposter syndrome?"
* When I must do the mix-and-mingle thing, as I like to stay with people I am comfortable with (I don't like small talk).
* I feel less intelligent when I am dealing with those who are in higher positions than me (like when I talk to powerful alumni), and I always feel like I must prove myself.
* Telling myself that I don't have a lot to offer, that I won't be taken seriously, and people won't like me.
* Having difficult conversations with teachers or parents as I prefer to avoid conflict.

Looking over her list showed me that her discomfort was essentially divided between internal negativity and having to engage with people in person and lead the conversation. So I asked which was the most difficult for her. She said it was all hard. I hear this a lot but not all distractions are super derailers, so it is important to push past this initial roadblock to find out what truly gets in the way.

To get Cameron thinking I asked a few specifics: Was it uncomfortable to walk in the room appearing composed, or was introducing yourself to people the culprit? Once you started a conversation were you able to settle into your role as a lead organizer?

Now she had something to say. Her most pressing obstacles to performing to her standards were escalating self-criticism as the event neared, particularly traveling to the event and waiting for people to arrive, and the uncertainty of how to initially engage with people in a relaxed manner. She noted that she strongly resisted moving around the room to interact with new people as she much preferred to stay with those she knew or those with whom she was already talking. Cameron wanted strategies to ease her entry into these social situations.

Ty the NFL Quarterback:
"I hate conflict"

Ty found his coach to be overly critical and contentious. Ty was young, laid-back, and looking to please his bosses. He was modest, unassuming, and in his words, "very nonconfrontational." He was good with his teammates; he would talk to them one-on-one when things went wrong rather than call them out to embarrass them. He was easygoing but was increasingly frustrated that his coach was negative and critical no matter how he played. Ty remarked, "I make a great play and all he says is 'Don't throw crappy passes,' or 'Make sure you have two hands on the ball.' I can't help but think, *Really*, thanks for the helpful feedback."

As an NFL quarterback, and a large and imposing human, people expected Ty to be aggressive by nature, to be demanding and forceful and unfazed by physical violence, verbal confrontation, or hard criticism. He was tough on the field, but Ty was a sensitive person and loved a harmonious environment, so his distractions were not surprising:

* Getting results—will I be able to satisfy this guy (coach)?
* Coach forcing me to stay too tightly bound to his directives and a system in a game, not allowing me to adjust in the moment to make a play that I see unfolding.

* Making mistakes (I then overdo it because I am trying to make up for it).
* Coach always worrying about my completion percentage.
* Coach being overly negative and critical. I am logical and already self-critical enough.
* When the coach doesn't give me credit for my good performances.
* Teammates who dawdle and show up late.

When we went over his list, I asked Ty to be more specific about which of his coach's comments bothered him the most. He said that his coach was always on him to play like some of the top quarterbacks in the league. "Of course, they are great quarterbacks, but I don't play like them, so I won't be my best if I try to copy them. I want to play like me and use my strengths. My coach is too stifling, he is holding me back and I don't know what to do."

Ty's super derailers boiled down to when the coach wanted him to play like a robot, or someone else ("I like structure but don't want to be bound. I want to be able to adjust on the fly on the field depending on what is happening"), and the unease he felt about how to talk to his coach!

Ty needed to decide for himself how he wanted to play. Then he had to prepare himself to act and confront the coach with his own ideas about how he should lead the team on the field. Ty was sure the coach would push back loud and hard on his ideas, so we worked on how to manage that next meeting.

Alex the Tennis Star:
"I could have fought harder for it"

I was watching a high-level junior tennis tournament when a coach asked me to speak with his player. Alex, the seventeen-year-old top prospect, had always been a fantastic performer and never seemed to waver, no matter the match or opponent. However, over the last year the coach was seeing that Alex was not as resilient to the pressures of performing. This is of course to be expected when one continues to move up the competition ladder. What feels easy at fifteen can suddenly feel onerous and difficult as the talent pool sharpens. A year before, Alex was able to play at a high level anytime, any-where, against anyone. She naturally connected to the technical execution of each stroke, and "went for" her shots no matter the score. As she matured into the next age category, Alex started to feel pressure to get results. She wanted to be a big success on the professional tennis circuit. She saw first-hand how good she had to be (which she already was, whether she knew it or not) and was seeing the importance of having a clear and controlled head. She had never had to think her way through her performances.

As is the nature of the unique business of performance psychology, Alex and I met in the only somewhat private place we could find, a stair-well. As we started listing her hot spots, it became clear she was thinking too much about the end of the match while she was still in it:

* Results, as in getting points and improving my ranking.
* When I hit the ball into the net, that really bothers me.
* When I think I should be playing better.
* When I am playing well, I suddenly worry that my opponent may start to play better.
* When I feel tense, nervous, or anxious I start making mistakes and get self-critical, so I start to hold back. I don't like that.
* I worry about what others may be thinking. I look to my coach in the stands too much when things aren't going well.
* When I get frustrated or angry, I focus on my opponent's game and forget about mine.
* When my expectations are high and I really want to beat someone.
* When I am too quiet on the court, I am in my head think-ing too much and not playing my game.

Alex played the next day, so it was important to help her organize this list of distractions. To prevent her from feeling overwhelmed, I wanted to make sure we went directly to the most pressing issues and leave the rest for later. I wanted her to just pick out the two or three things that were most likely to go wrong (if anything would) against this particular opponent. I pointed out that her list showed a tendency to worry excessively about her opponents. I am watchful for this possibility as too many players (and teams) prioritize studying the trends and minutiae of their competitors' game over their own. Being ready to defend against or attack another is smart preparation, but the most important game is your game. Alex needed to make her competitor deal with her strengths and her tactics, knowing that if she stuck to her own game she would play well.

In addition to overthinking her opponent, Alex's biggest blocks were when she hit the ball into the net (this particular error aggravated her greatly, increasing her vulnerability to further unforced errors) and being too quiet during play (verbally and physically), leaving her feeling tense and flat, diminishing her usual overpowering force on the court.

Jamie the Investment Manager:
"When I get tense and emotional, I say things I regret"

Jamie had recently finished his MBA and was working at a big bank in capital markets. He had a good job with enormous opportunities to advance, lots of friends, and a great new girlfriend. When we met, he said he wanted to "get control" of himself, to finally be honest and confront his bad behavior. Jamie was defensive and could be volatile. He knew if it continued, he would jeopardize his job and his close relationships.

It was clear he was an intense, restless person. He was also funny, excitable, and creative. He was easily bored so he loved change and variety.

He was very sensitive to criticism and said, "When I face any type of adversity or failure, I crumble." Jamie wanted to be able to fight through the crumbling and "not be a jerk anymore." When feeling emotional or anxious, he wanted to learn how to avoid defaulting to shouting and making condescending or self-protective remarks. He was tired of having to repair the ruptures he was needlessly creating. Jamie said he was at his worst when:

* I let myself be a moody hothead.
* I am criticized at work, or anywhere actually.
* I feel monotony, like having to do routine or administrative work.
* I experience a really slow work pace or delays.
* I feel threatened or attacked, and then I withdraw.
* I get or give the silent treatment.
* I face any type of adversity or failure, and crumble.
* I am doling out cutting or disrespectful remarks, and I know I am losing control.
* I am feeling hurt and insecure.
* I get pulled into negative group think.
* I am intolerant and lacking empathy.
* I talk too much, and I know I am not listening.
* I am getting too tense or wound up.
* I am defensive.
* I overcomplicate things.
* I don't want to look weak.

Jamie had no problem identifying his biggest derailer, which was criticism from anyone. "I don't handle it well, it hurts me. My dad used to criticize me as a kid. I could feel his disappointment even as a nine-year-old when I didn't make the ten-year-old team." When his boss gave him feedback on a project or task, constructive or not, Jamie immediately interpreted the comments as critical. He assumed that his work wasn't good enough, triggering his anger. He would let this inappropriate and petulant behavior ramp up very quickly and it always made him feel weak. He would inflame his shame further by telling himself that he didn't need anybody, or that he would quit his job. Whenever he felt threatened, he would push people away. He was looking for a way to rearrange his impetuous reactions. "I want to be more respectful and reliable; I want to be a good man."

———

Step 1, identifying your super derailers, doesn't take long, but it's vitally important. Once you've identified them, it's time for the next step in the process: applying strategies to manage these concerns in the moment, when you're under pressure and need to stay focused. My top four skills are presented over the next four chapters, and we'll see how each client develops and uses them.

Chapter Twelve

Skill 1:
Get Calm and Stay There

I love this skill. I talk about it all the time to anyone who will listen. If I was only allowed to pick one skill to tell my clients to practice, this would be it. Whether you are an opera singer, an executive negotiating a jumbo deal, or a teacher dealing with an impertinent student, you have to be able to cool it. Being able to soothe yourself, even a little, will let you focus on performing well (or at least better) in that moment. Being able to calm down in important situations will enhance your actions and the outcome. You will not achieve your best if you can't settle yourself.

Unchecked tension makes it difficult to get calm, much less stay calm. Tension is that feeling of worry, nervousness, or unease that clouds your thinking and tightens your body. That tension can instantly obliterate your performance. Blasting out of the starting blocks a fraction of a second before the starter's signal will disqualify an Olympic sprinter. That is tension at work. Driving home on the highway and suddenly finding yourself shouting at another driver when he speeds past. This too is tension muscling its way into your space, likely from some other upset earlier in your day. A team owner constantly telling his experienced but now beleaguered coaching staff how to coach and whom to play (even during games), all the while insisting that he isn't "the anxious type." I've seen that too. Tension can become a monster and will humble anyone, even those who won't admit it! But you can learn to tune your tension and manage pressure through a calmer, more agile mind.

How tense is too tense? That depends on you. Thinking back to your quality performances, the ones you were happy with, simply rate your tension during those games, recitals, or meetings. On a scale of 1 to 10, 1 being calm and loose and 10 being nervous or tight, how tense were you? Most people will say anywhere from 1 to 3 but I think anything under 5 works just fine. Once your tension starts to creep into the 6 and 7 range, the mental clutter mounts. Anything past an 8 is hard to come back from. Nobody is comfortable or does their best work at this end of the scale. That is why it is important to check in with yourself before and during the event.

When you notice that you have hit 6, you need to bring it back down, fast. Once you hit that range, your heart rate elevates, you breathe too fast and too much, your decision-making and timing suffers, your muscles tighten up, your precision is off, you may become reactive, forget an important comment, or the next step in solving a problem. You may become more passive and hesitant or impatient and frustrated. You won't be fully focused. You will get in your own way by forcing things, taking too many uncalculated risks, or moving too much without purpose (e.g., always trying to smash the ball when you are at the net on the pickleball court no matter the situation, or over-striding around the stage during your TED Talk). A surgeon I worked with commented that when he felt his tension rise beyond his comfort zone, his tactile performance was affected and he couldn't manipulate his equipment as smoothly as usual. Too much tension is distracting and limits your output.

What about too little tension? Can you be too relaxed to perform optimally? Occasionally a new client will insist that being "too relaxed" is their performance issue. I have yet to be convinced. Blaming a poor performance on being a naturally calm and cool person, one who takes life as it comes and doesn't get stressed about much, admittedly feels much better than facing the fact that you were unprepared, anxious, or too afraid to try. The reality is you just weren't ready. Whether you noticed or not, your tension got too high, and you backed off. Maybe you felt tired, lazy,

or unenthusiastic but misread those feelings as disinterest rather than tension. Perhaps you didn't recognize that you felt overwhelmed or resigned,
which typically makes a person say things like "I don't care" or "It doesn't
matter." Under pressure, you do care and it does matter.

Tension can cause chaos and drama, and crush you if you let it. Great
performances under pressure come with less tension—not zero tension,
just a level that you can tolerate and still stay in the moment (or reclaim
the moment if you lose it). Know your tension threshold, know your
number, and make a serious effort to keep it in your comfort zone. How?
Start with your breath.

Breathing is a natural sedative and is undervalued as a tool for managing the tension that pressure creates. It sounds goofy to some, but the most
efficient way to get calm is to pay attention to your breathing. I mentioned
this during a corporate health and wellness summit and a clearly irritated
woman piped up and said, "Oh no! Are you going to tell me that breathing will change my life?" She obviously thought my enthusiasm was flaky.
It isn't. Proper breathing can help you cope with stress, sleep better, be less
angry or moody, and refresh your energy. It can slow your heart rate and
reduce your blood pressure. This isn't speculation: There is excellent medical
and psychological research on how breathwork not only influences our immune response and eases chronic pain but can also help maintain and restore
health in general, both physical and mental. I wanted to tell her all of that!
But less is often more, so I simply replied that "Breathing will allow you to
settle enough so you can focus on what you need to do to be better, and at
the very least you can use breathing to prevent you from freaking out. Let
me show you what might help." Happily, for me, she was game to at least try.

It isn't hard, doesn't take long, and you can do it anywhere. No matter
how busy you are, you can make time for this skill.

Sit down, get comfortable, and breathe normally for one minute. Don't
try anything fancy, just count the exhalations you make during this time.
Stop here please! Do not read on until you have done this part of the exercise.

Now, we're going to breathe again for another minute but slower, exhaling longer and more fully. Breathe from your diaphragm, not your chest. To check if you are doing this, put your hand on your lower abdomen. As you inhale, feel your abdomen move outward. Let it expand so you can take a full breath. Breathe in through your nose and out through your nose as well. A note about exhalation: When you feel you have exhaled everything, keep going! Use your core to squeeze out a little bit more until your lungs feel empty. Imagine sinking or melting into your seat. During this minute, when you drift to other thoughts, gently bring your focus back to your breathing. Now try it please, counting your breaths again.

Compare your breath counts for each round. Most people normally breathe about eighteen times a minute, which is likely similar to the number of exhalations in your first minute. During the second round, breathing as suggested, I suspect your count was much lower. When you are breathing "properly" you will exhale about six to ten times a minute. You will feel more calm, loose, and relaxed. Breathing and emotions are connected. When people are angry, upset, or frustrated, how do they breathe? Their breaths are shallow and faster than usual. They will over-breathe through their mouths. They will huff and be noisy. They are not cool and calm. But when you are in control of your emotional state, your breaths are regular. They are in through your nose: slower, softer, and quiet. You can't be in control of your breathing and still be upset! Breathing properly helps you manage your tension and emotions, so you can cope with the pressure you will face.

Breathing is so easy but how we do it matters. The big idea here is to breathe through your nose and exhale *big*. Breathing properly activates your diaphragm, increases your lung capacity, and allows you to get more oxygen with each breath. Of course, we breathe through our mouths when talking or exercising hard, or when stressed and not paying attention to a healthy breathing pattern, but using your nose is more efficient and productive so do it often. If you are going to breathe out through your mouth, try using pursed lips (like you are breathing out of a straw) to slow it down. We are so conditioned to think about taking deep breaths, yet big breaths through the mouth only encourage rushed, short, stressed breaths from your chest. Think about breathing slower, softer, and longer. Relaxed and effortless breathing quiets our mental chatter and helps to align our emotions with our bodies. And it all starts with your nose.

All my clients do breathwork. Some are initially skeptical but end up discovering its benefits. A skier client of mine, who was in Europe for World Cup races, recently said to me, "You know, that breathing thing really works. I have used it in the last two races and my results qualified me for the Olympics! Breathing consciously in the start is allowing me to stay focused on the 'ski stuff' during the race. I didn't get distracted with worries about making a mistake or what my results might be." Then she added that a few days before, she felt tightness in her chest and thought she had COVID like others on the race circuit. "But then I sat down and took the time to breathe properly for a minute. It made me feel loose and fine. I didn't have COVID, I was just a little anxious about everything (including COVID) and didn't realize my tension had crept up on me."

It is so important to Breathe It Out. This is the one exercise that I ask all my clients to rely on as an in-the-moment go-to strategy. It doesn't take skill or toughness or confidence, you just have to decide to Breathe It Out when you need to.

Here it is in its simplicity: Breathe through your nose, breathe slower (which means less), exhale fully, and loosen your shoulders. Do it for a minute, or even ten seconds—it will help.

This is the breathing that the World Cup skier uses at the top of the Dolomites or the French Alps when she is about to explode out of the start and down a mountain. Runners use it during a race when the fatigue starts to tighten them up and shorten their strides. Surgeons use it when a complication suddenly arises in the operating room. Anybody can use it in their quest for self-control. You can use it in preparation for a particular situation or *during* a situation. Breathing It Out works anywhere, anytime. Practice it daily. One cycle of this breathing can be enough to settle you, but you can do it as many times as you need to lower your tension, even just a little. It literally only takes seconds.

Sometimes you need an extra boost to help manage your tension before performing. Listening to music or socializing with colleagues or teammates can calm your mind and relax your body. And during a performance, talking with teammates helps people stay loose and focused. Most athletes have a routine physical warm-up they use to make sure they are energized. On days when they are feeling a little tired or mentally flat, they may do a little more or do it for a little longer to get sharp. Musicians I talk to incorporate exercises to activate their fingers and hands before a concert; they may even walk up and down a flight of stairs to dissipate some building tension. Surgeons I know will warm up physically by squeezing a ball to enhance blood flow in their hands for mobility and a good sense of "feel." One sometimes dances alongside her scrub nurse while listening to music before surgery. Another makes sure he is fueled and hydrated to maintain an even keel for long procedures. Anything that helps them be ready to go.

I talk to all my clients about being able to Breathe It Out, as this skill will help them the most when they need it the most. Some need to work up to this benchmark so I give them one or two more exercises based on their attention span, how meditative they are by nature, or their interest level. The exercises have to suit the person, their character, and the time they have or want to invest. There are many options out there. You can listen to an app to guide your breathwork (following instructions is an easy way to start), watch a YouTube video, or read through an exercise before trying it on your own. But you must be able to Breathe It Out!

This is why each of our performers has this exercise in their breathwork repertoire. And each uses a variety of breathwork that's right for them. Try each to see what feels comfortable for you.

Riley

Riley was fast-paced and always thinking. His tendency to lose his focus or jump from one thought quickly to the next made it clear that a variety of short exercises would be the best fit for him and that guided breathing would be the easiest way to start.

EXHALE FIRST. Riley tended to breathe fast and shallow, so he threw this exercise into his day. People tend to think all about their inhaling when they try to consciously breathe. They take a big breath in and this often leads to a shallow breath (not using your diaphragm), a tight chest, and feeling a little dizzy. To deliver more oxygen to your brain and body, first sit tall. Think about your exhalation as the start of your breathing cycle. Then, focus on your breath, let it happen (through your nose) without trying to change it.

SLOW IT DOWN. This exercise was app-based and brief at two minutes long. Slow, smooth breathing using a 4-2-4 pattern. Take a slow, easy breath in (through your nose) for a count of four seconds, then hold for two, then out (through your nose) for four. Repeat five or six times, more if you want. Notice how your body has relaxed and released tension. Riley used this daily and throughout the day, such as before getting out of the car when he arrived at the rink.

BREATHE IT OUT. Now that Riley knew how to breathe efficiently, he was ready to practice this exercise throughout the day. Breathe slow, exhale fully (as you continue to exhale, tighten your core to push a little more air out), loosen your shoulders. Repeat for a few cycles if you have time. Riley did this on his way to the rink for practice or for games, during drills at practice while he was waiting in line, before he warmed up for a game, and on the bench between shifts.

WARM UP HARDER. In addition to breathing, Riley needed to better tune his tension on game days. He added an extra ten minutes to his pregame bike warm-up in the gym. This helped him push through any physical tightness and nagging worries that were fueled by anxiety and how he would play. As a result of the breathing and biking, he felt more relaxed and able to start the game at a high level rather than use the first few shifts to ease into the game. He knew if he wasn't primed to start, a bad first shift or two could easily convince his coach to reduce his ice time.

As an additional exercise to tune his tension we added a sleep plan.

Although not a super derailer, Riley wanted to address the fact that during the season he often had trouble falling asleep or getting back to sleep. As a highly energized person, he found himself overstimulated with mind noise. His overthinking could be related to a good or bad performance, feedback, or unresolved feelings not processed during the day. He'd put these thoughts on hold until they came pushing forward at night, uninvited. The plan was simple:

Later in the Day (Before Dinner):

* Breathe, do a quick review of your facts list (we'll learn about these in chapter 14). Make sure you evaluated your practice or last game. Write out your plan for tomorrow. Add any other tasks that are on your mind to help park them for the moment. On game nights evaluate your performance afterward, or do it first thing the next day.

Before Bed:

* Take time to wind down, go to bed gradually, dim lights thirty minutes before bed, and get off your devices. Breathe through your nose, slow with a long exhale. Read something light. Fiction works!

In Bed:

* Settle down and do the "exhale first" exercise (while lying down). Slow it down and exhale longer, think about loose, soft legs and arms, relax your jaw, and sink into the mattress. Surrender to sleep and let go of waking rather than fight the worry of not getting to sleep. If you really can't sleep just rest gently or get out of bed and go read.

Cameron

Cameron was naturally tense and meticulous. She liked to do things "right." So I suggested a longer exercise (five minutes rather than two) that would give her a little extra time to relax her whole body. When learning full-body relaxation, many people are told to first tense then release different body parts in a progression from their feet to their head in an effort to experience the difference between feeling tension and relaxation. I have found that almost everyone knows what tension feels like if they take a moment to check in with their body. For Cameron, I didn't want her to double down on the tension part of the exercise as she was tense enough, so I went with the relaxation part only.

BODY MELT. Sit or lie down, get comfortable, close your eyes, and drop your shoulders. Breathe smoothly, in and out through your nose. The idea here is to slowly scan your body and practice relaxing your muscles. Start with your feet, feel them go limp and droopy. Take a couple of easy breaths before you move on to the next body part. Then do the same with your legs, your stomach, shoulders, arms, and hands. Let each body part relax and think about sinking into your chair or melting into the surface you are comfortably lying on. Finish with softening your face and jaw. Keep breathing as long as you like, then slowly open your eyes.

BREATHE IT OUT. Cameron was now more aware and in control of her tension level and wanted to increase her ability to calm herself in the moment. She practiced breathing it out a couple of times a day (while walking down the hall or going to refill her water bottle), always several times on the way to a formal social event for the school, and again just before introducing herself to new or important guests at the event. Cameron came to love this exercise as it is discreet so she could do it without anyone realizing.

POSTURE. Lastly, to address tension when at an event, Cameron made sure to relax her body by reminding herself to stand tall and check that her shoulders were down and out of her ears! When she felt calmer, she felt others responded well.

Ty

Ty was steady and tolerant. He was good at staying cool except when he anticipated a conflict. The bigger the potential conflict the more risk-averse he became. He needed to be more assertive with his coach about his tactical ideas but worried his coach would perceive it as a challenge and he very much wanted to avoid a contentious interaction. He knew he had to purposefully settle down going into the meeting as his breathing would be rushed and up in his chest, clouding his trademark calm. All he had to do was be mindful of his breathing.

BREATHE IT OUT. Ty practiced his breathing for a couple of days. He liked how quickly it made his mind feel clear. He even started to use it regularly during games, especially when the pressure was on.

SET THE TONE. At the meeting, Ty decided that this time he needed to set the tone. He wanted it to be open and inviting of discussion rather than rigid and uncompromising. To ensure this, he needed to start with his own behavior. As he walked out of the locker room and down the hall, he took those ten seconds to breathe it out. As he turned into the meeting room, he stood up to his full six-four height, looked his coach in the eye, and took a moment to smile his easy smile. He told himself to sit down, lean back, and keep his feet on the floor (so he did not let tension jiggle his leg up and down). This was enough to loosen Ty up and start talking.

Alex

As a seasoned athlete even at seventeen, Alex knew she was supposed to breathe for performance power. But she kept forgetting to do it when she really needed to, when things weren't going her way. Her impression of "breathing" was that she had to sit for twenty minutes and listen to bird-songs (which can be nice) or some fluffy motivational platitudes about becoming her epic self (which I agreed was not particularly useful or enduring). I laughed with admiration as this kid wanted a direct line to what she needed to fix, now.

BREATHE IT OUT. We were both happy to skip any filler and I suggested we go right to breathing it out, to the action that would immediately subdue any sign of her emotional fragility on the court. Alex liked the brevity and the results this provided; she knew this skill would allow her to reassemble her approach when she was drifting. At various times she used this breathing before she warmed up for a match, between points, between games, during changeovers, and before she served. She also used it to reset when she was frustrated or not playing well. To give herself time to breathe it out, she would walk a little slower to her towel box to wipe her racquet grip or her hands. She wasn't stalling, she simply wasn't rushing. On big match days she would check in with herself and breathe it out regularly, from the time she woke up to the end of her match: one round of this breathing won't suffice when facing the big moments. Alex came off the court after a giant win and said, "All I did was breathe the whole time, I can't believe I had to do it so often, but it was worth it!" If you have to do it every fifteen minutes during the day or fifty times during an event, then do it.

FUEL UP. Alex used other strategies to get calm and stay there. On competition days she was nervous and often skipped eating. She had to make sure she fueled up properly. She learned to make herself eat something a few hours before her match and then keep hydrating and eating small bites during the match.

STRETCH. She also made sure to stretch a little more to release lingering tension and liked to do the Ragdoll (yoga pose) to end her warm-up. She stood tall, then gently folded forward at her hips and let her hands fall toward the court, loosely swaying and shaking herself out, then stood and rolled her shoulders out and down. Now she was ready to take another shot at playing well and moving up the rankings.

Jamie

If Jamie was ever going to get a handle on his low impulse control, he had to learn to manage his breathing. He would not be able to curb his defensive behavior if he couldn't slow down his breath. He would need an exercise that could quickly bring his racing thoughts and pounding heart rate under control. Learning to harness the power of exhaling fully would allow him to move his diaphragm and push more air out so he could take more in, slowing his breath and calming his body.

4-7-8 BREATHING. This exercise is excellent as an antianxiety remedy. You can use it before you react to something or just to feel less stressed. I pulled up one of the many online links to this breathing and Jamie followed along. That was all it took for him to be able to practice this method himself.

Once you sit down and get settled, close your mouth and inhale quietly through your nose for a count of four, hold your breath for a count of seven, and then exhale through your mouth with pursed lips (like you are breathing through a straw) for a count of eight. Keep this ratio as the exhalation should be twice that of the inhalation. Repeat this cycle four times. This is great for fending off rising intensity and panic. Jamie practiced this consciously to put himself in a more relaxed state and stop an impending impulsive reaction.

BREATHE IT OUT. Once he was comfortable with the 4-7-8 breathing, Jamie added breathing it out for those go-to moments when he needed to connect to his breath in a more discreet manner, such as before meeting with his boss, or when he felt anger building or a criticism coming. Less tension meant he wasn't starting with his back up, ready to defend himself or be verbally sharp to someone. Less tension allowed him to pull himself back, to wait and react with more control.

Tweak your breathing. We should all be practicing our breathing daily, not only for physical health but emotional balance. A calmer mind and a relaxed body move through pressure with less restriction and more energy.

We can add to this loosened state, even amid tension, by going for a walk. Go for a stroll around your house, outside your office, or wherever your performance is taking place, and dawdle a bit.

Putter about for a minute or ten and let your mind go wherever it wants without trying to corral it. Look around, check out the skyline, or that painting you like, or the cute dog sprawled out on the carpet. Let yourself be distracted so you are not bothered by your usual distractions, which is ironically calming. Yes, you want to be focused for a task, but enjoy a mindless meander before you need to be more mindful. This little bit of directionlessness brings a valuable reset.

All it takes to get calm and stay there is keeping our tension and breathing in check. It's that simple. There are plenty of good breathing exercises out there and I encourage you to think about what sort of exercise would help you most (long or short, guided or not). But everyone benefits from breathing it out in the moment, when it matters most. And our next skill focuses on those crucial performance moments.

Chapter Thirteen

Skill 2:
Forget How You Feel, It's About What You Do

Experience or skill or both, even at a high level, doesn't immunize you from middling or failed performances. Too often when people struggle, they let how they feel override what they should be doing. They assume they have suddenly "lost it" and must wait out the slump that they somehow have no control over.

This isn't true. Barring illness or injury, in most cases "it" is right there where they left it. They haven't lost their skill, but they do need to find their focus. They need to remember that while confidence is all about how you feel, performing is all about what you do—and the best way to perform is to know precisely how to act in the moment.

Be ready to think. But wait, haven't we all been told repeatedly that thinking gets in the way of performing? That you should just get out there and let it happen? So often I hear "I always do my best when I am not thinking" or "I overthink too much and want to learn to stop!" My advice is: Do not do this, it does not work. As a strategy, "don't think" is both unrealistic and unreliable. Of course, on those good days when your tension is automatically low and you are fully focused on the task, not on potential problems, let it ride. But be ready to think.

It may feel counterintuitive, but whether you are feeling good or bad or tired or scared, it literally does not matter in the moment. What matters are your skills not your emotions.

A former MLB player recently sat in on a talk I gave to professional players about feelings, thinking, and doing. As we left the meeting, walking and talking down the hall, he was reflective and thoughtful. "I didn't realize it when I was a player, but I always did the *do* that you were just talking about. I never told myself, 'Don't do that.' I always told myself what to do to execute well. I felt every at-bat was a big moment and to minimize the emotions I felt under this pressure I somehow simplified my thinking and focused on the one thing I needed to do that would give me the best chance to hit the ball, whether it was to 'get my foot down' or get my 'hands out front.' It was a big deal for me to make the big leagues, so I never thought I was talented. I guess I surprised myself. I won a major league batting title because I could get past my feelings and think about what to *do* in the moment. I thought out there. I did the *do*."

How do you do the *do*? Performance cues are my strategy of choice. They are what you need to complete the task well. Performance cues are those words or phrases that prompt you to act at the right time in the right way. Being able to literally tell yourself what to do is vital to performing well. The most effective performance cues are usually technical or tactical in nature and key in on the more difficult aspects of what you are trying to accomplish, on the "tough bits" rather than the actions you do automatically. Under pressure, they direct you to proper (or at least good enough) execution, or to emphasize part of a sequence or finish strong; it all depends on your need or weakness. Either way, they keep you on track and away from disorganized thoughts.

Performance cues work for everyone. I was on the phone with an F-18 fighter pilot talking about landing on "the boat" (an aircraft carrier) at 160 miles per hour, in the dark. I mentioned that there must be a distraction or two that pop up while executing this exacting maneuver. Her response was, "It is all about getting into the box [your "good day" mental box] so distractions can't get to you. My only focus is on what I am doing." In this scenario, her performance cues or phrases are the very specific "boat" procedures that are exhaustively drilled into every pilot.

What happens when distractions do get in the way? In primary flight school she once felt herself struggling to stay in her "good day" mental box. As she was taking off on a flight that was being graded, her instructor pilot pointedly asked, "Why are you here? Nobody wants you. Nobody wants you in the fleet." As an early female Marine pilot, she knew very well that some individuals would be confrontational, but this guy desperately wanted to see her fail. "He did rattle me a little, so I first had to decide that my lack of focus was unacceptable, and it had to stop." This self-directive was psychologically superior. She was immediately sharp and direct with herself; she didn't whine to herself about the injustice of the situation or look for excuses to justify a potentially poor performance. She continued, "That way, I could get back to what I was supposed to be doing and mentally move to focusing on the technical precision of the maneuvers I was to perform. I always prepared well and was mentally ready to manage the stress he was trying to stir up as I had my maneuvers and any related key technical cues written down on my kneeboard card [that is strapped to the pilot's leg] for reference." She ignored the instructor pilot's contemptible comments calculated to block her advancement (rather than develop pilot toughness and problem-solving under duress) and expertly shifted back to her assignments, on what she had to *do* to succeed on that flight. She could deal with this coward later.

It's good to think while performing but you need to know the rules. Mine are simple. Your cues must be precise, they need to tell your body what to do (rather than what not to do) or your mind where to go, and there can only be a few.

I am relentless when working through cues with clients because when I initially ask what they do when they are performing well, they often talk in ineffective generalities. "I compete hard," "I don't think" (yes you do, but you are not aware and probably occupied, at least partially, with distracting mental clutter), "I stand my ground," "I am myself out there," "I challenge my opponent," "I feel confident" (when under pressure I don't care how you feel, I care what you do!)—you get the idea. None of these broader ideas or self-directives tell me *how* you will become aggressive or *what* actions will lead to "being yourself."

While broader statements like these can provide a solid philosophical starting point for your approach, if you don't drill down further you won't find the cues that will actually keep you on top of your mechanics, stay in your flow, or help you fight back from mistakes. Drilling down lets you take your focus a step further, to understand the exact space where you tend to go wrong. Drill down until you recognize the tough bits, the areas that scare you physically or psychologically, the procedures or parts of the sequence or presentation that are not automatic.

As you refine your skills and improve your moves, adjust your cues to continue to target the elements of the performance you want to get right. Fix one issue and then move on to the next challenge until you are satisfied with your approach. One client started to climb the world squash rankings after she drilled down and applied cues to progressively more difficult situations. First, she had to gain consistency with a couple of her weaker shots, then she wanted to stay calmer when playing in big tournaments. After that, she needed to stay focused when she was down in a game, then again when she was winning a game, and lastly when trying to close out the match. She kept pushing her limits and was doing great. Then I got the call. She had just lost in the semi-finals of an important tournament and was fuming: "I wanted to beat her so badly. Yes, she is good, but I know I can beat her. I let her get in my head!" She got caught up in her feelings and let the *do* slip away. Playing well against top-ranked players was the next test she needed to face.

So we did some drilling. She watched video of her last match and we talked. She realized that long rallies were her current obstacle. The longer the rally the more invested she became in winning the point (or losing it). The escalating anticipation of victory or defeat with every shot intensified her tension and impeded her execution. Long rallies against the *big girls* made her panic as she knew if she hit a loose ball or made two mistakes in a row that they would punish her quickly and harshly. "To work so hard for eight or ten shots and win the point, it is so exhilarating and motivating. But it really hurts to lose them. When I stop thinking about the process, I think only about winning or losing and that is a problem." We had to figure out how she could better protect her investment as she went deeper into those rallies against the world's best.

Here is what she decided: Once she had hit six or seven shots in the rally, she knew she had to buckle down, engage her mind, and stay loose. She would override her mental drift by keeping her "shoulders down" and telling herself to throw up a "soft shot" so she could feel suppleness and control in her hands (and not mindlessly bang balls off the wall) and get her opponent to the back of the court to give herself a moment to regroup. She spent the next five days mentally practicing that scenario in anticipation of her upcoming match at the US Open. She lost in a long close battle at the very end because, as she explained to me, she wandered away from the process and immersed herself in the potential results. She knew she needed to stick with her cues until she repaired her approach to long rallies. She was still fuming but was moving in the right direction and we both knew there was more success to come.

What if you find yourself randomly or endlessly changing your well-planned cues? If you do, be aware that this is not a diligent or sincere search for the answer and more likely resistance to putting yourself to the test. Moving casually from one cue to the next with no useful effect may feel like you are closing in on success but more likely you are protecting yourself from finding out whether you can do it. Perpetually hovering around the possibility of success can feel less painful than risking the misery of failure. The irony is that if you follow through with your cues you put yourself in the best position to get the results you are looking for. Reaching for more can be a tough thing to do, so when selecting your cues be precise, tell your body what to do, and have only a few. And then use them. This is how you solve tough performance problems.

When evaluating your performances, you have to be brave and honest to find the right cues. It's something Sammy, a starting baseball catcher, had to quickly learn to get his game back on track. At this particular minor league stadium where I visited him, the only way to get to the dugout was through the clubhouse, which in baseball is where players shower, change, and hang out. I asked if the coast was clear and a player shouted, "Guys! Put your wieners away! Dana is coming through!" Head down and red-faced, I scooted through the room and as I was almost out the other end, Sammy stopped me and said, "I'm embarrassed." I looked up and said, "Uh, yeah, me too!" "No, I mean I keep dropping pop-ups and I am struggling. I don't know how to fix it, and this is keeping me from getting to the big leagues."

Before practice that day, Sammy sat me down in the empty stands and it all tumbled out, how his anxiety skyrocketed with each ball he dropped. Coaches had tried to help him with countless drills and encouragement, but nothing was working. Teammates and coaches were now making jokes and betting on the ball hitting the ground. I could hear his distress and felt his anguish, but I avoided his feelings for the moment. Instead, I asked him to teach me how to catch a pop-up.

"I never think about how to do it, I just do it," he said. "Well, that's the problem," I told him. "It isn't going very well, and I know you can fix this, so please stand up and show me." He began by telling me, "I guess I run to the ball." "Yes," I said, "but what is the first thing you are supposed to do?" "Oh yeah, I take off my mask." Then he got rolling through the sequence of required actions and came up with five points. First, you remove your mask; then find the ball and move to the area in which you anticipate the ball will come down; next, turn your back to the infield because the spin will bring the ball back to the mound and you will be in a better position to catch it; then use two hands to secure the catch; and finally, if runners are on base you turn to make the next play. We were drilling down, and he was getting precise. He wasn't talking about how he was feeling—he was all about the *do*.

We needed to identify which steps were going wrong. I asked him, "What isn't automatic, what is the tough bit, which one aren't you doing?" He wasn't immediately sure but as he acted out the steps several times he realized that his anxiety kicked in as soon as the ball was popped up. He would then sprint to the ball. I asked, "What should you be doing in that moment, as in what do you need to do to actually catch the ball?" "I need to move slowly to the ball as I have a lot more time than I think I do." He had been rushing because he was feeling anxious. His attention then jumped ahead to the result, to whether he would catch the ball or not, encouraging more tension and distraction.

He roughed out his new cues in practice that afternoon and decided that he needed to slowly find the ball as he didn't have to go far. Previously, when the ball was in the air, he would panic and get into a full conversation with himself in those few seconds. His thoughts could range from something as simple as "Don't drop it" to "You are a pro, just catch it." He decided that in the game that night, as soon as a pop-up was hit, he would tell himself to "go SLOW" and move slowly to the ball.

When he caught the first one that night the formerly compassionless dugout went wild for him. Sammy's relief was "massive," and his coach even told him he was proud of him (which was monumental on its own). He quickly ended his pop-up struggle all because he thought through his dilemma with precision and clarity.

Not long after, he made it to the pros. In fact, he was half of one of the best pitcher-catcher partnerships going in Major League Baseball and enjoyed a long career. It is amazing what you can do for yourself when you change your cues from "Oh no, I can't catch these things" to "Slow down, I have time." Sammy stuck with the *do*. You can too.

When you select your cues, start by taking a moment to review your good performances. Capture all the actions or the technical elements that allowed you to excel. You will get a chance later to condense them for your performances, but for now list a bunch, as our five performance case studies did.

Riley

Once Riley focused on what he was doing on the ice when things were going well, settling on his top performance cues was easy:

*   Move my feet.
*   Keep skating (start/stop or north/south, no circling around!).
*   Hard first three strides.
*   Hold on to the puck.
*   Go to open ice.
*   Make sure I finish my checks (put my shoulder into him, bump him).
*   Get up on the forecheck.
*   Stay low.
*   Strong on my stick.
*   Shoot, shoot, shoot!

When he's focusing on these actions, he has a much better chance of *doing* them as he's not thinking about his ice time, his stats, or any other distractions. His cues shift him away from his distractions.

Cameron

Whether on her way to an event or during the event itself, Cameron knew if she kept attending to her cues, she would manage her performance with more ease:

*   Breathe, breathe, and breathe again.
*   Scan my body to loosen, release my shoulders.
*   Hands by sides or in front (arms not crossed).
*   Start with someone familiar (to get my groove) but then move to someone new.
*   Walk slower, move from person to person with purpose (rather than end up wandering trying to look busy).
*   Initiate, approach people at different tables, say hello, and always introduce myself with a smile.

* Look people in the eye.
* Ask questions, *listen* to the response.
* Stand when making a welcome toast (resist staying seated).
* Ten minutes max with one person then move on.

All of this is to prompt her to leave her comfort zone, to appear open and approachable rather than aloof. And these actions also ready her to focus on the conversation and connect properly.

Ty

Ty needed to push back on his more forceful coach if he wanted to lead himself and his team better. To avoid being passive and walking away from the meeting dissatisfied yet again (with himself and his coach), he took the time to structure the specific points he wanted to address. Then he pinpointed the cues that would help him perform:

* Write down my ideas (including what feedback helps me and what doesn't) and have the list with me.
* Say what I think, just get the words out.
* Stay on topic, keep coming back to my points until they are resolved in some way.
* Disagree if I disagree!
* Respond to force with calm, keep my composure, keep an even tone.
* It is a discussion, not a fight.

Ty started the meeting outlining what he liked about the coach's playbook and how the coach had made him a better player (which was true). He then said he had some possible refinements to run by the coach and a thought or two about what kind of feedback motivates (rather than deflates) him. Hard conversations can easily go off the rails, but Ty was learning how to start them well.

Alex

Once Alex started to think about what made her hard to play against and what her opponents didn't want to face, she easily listed her cues:

* Move my feet.
* Move to the ball.
* Get set up early for the ball.
* Get to the ball fast.
* Accelerate through the shot.
* Breathe out when I hit.
* Go to my towel to slow down.

These cues kept her playing in the moment and staying in the *do*, instead of worrying about what others were thinking about her.

Jamie

To increase patience, lessen self-criticism, and prevent damage to his relationships, Jamie knew he had to stick to his cues to avoid outbursts. When stressed or unsure he needed to listen more and talk less (or not at all). Only then could he begin to see a perspective other than his own:

* Shut up and hold my reaction.
* Sink into my seat and lean back slowly.
* If standing, keep my hands down and take a step back.

* If I can't hold it, suggest taking a break, walk away, and go gather myself.
* Shut up for five seconds and say nothing (the first thing he'd say was the worst thing).
* Stay down—stay seated or avoid making myself big because I feel vulnerable.
* Fix my face! Loosen it.

———

With your performance cues listed, you're halfway through the skills. Later, we'll revisit these to pick the most important, but for now there is another skill to look at, and it's fun once you get going.

Chapter Fourteen

Skill 3:
Talk Your Way Through It

Watch what you say to yourself. Self-talk can have a significant impact on how you feel and what you do. Modifying the chatter in your head to make it beneficial is an excellent mental pursuit, but to be clear, we're not talking about a list of affirmations repeated daily in front of the mirror (though you can do that if you wish), or something you'd see written on an inspirational poster. I am talking about examining your personal internal narrative and revising it to accurately reflect productive moments.

When talking about talk, I like to start with the facts, your facts. These are your accomplishments, those things you have achieved. Facts are real, the evidence of past successful or constructive performances. Facts are important because no one, not even you in a moment of doubt or fit of bad temper, can legitimately dismiss something you have achieved (even though you may try). Facts help you stay focused on what is true and real.

I was working with a young player at the French Open and in preparation for her singles match the next day we sat down in the players' lounge to fine-tune her game plan. I could see she was starting to get nervous (to be expected), and it quickly became clear she was indulging in negative scenarios in her head. So I went straight to the facts and asked what her tennis accomplishments were to date. She responded with "I don't know."

She was playing in the French Open! It's ridiculous that she could be there and not have accomplishments, and I told her so. Still, she said, "I don't have any." Her default response to go negative when feeling pressure was kicking in. I tried a different tack, reminding her of the facts.

"All the players here are good, yes? Well, this includes you, so tell me what makes you good, what you have done on the court, what you have accomplished to get yourself here." She hesitated so I started her off with a few basics I knew to be true. "Are you fit? Are you strong?" She reluctantly picked up the pen, but quickly wrote: "I played my way into this tournament with good results and for sure deserve to be here. I am a highly ranked player. I am fit, strong, and have a powerful game. I have shown my ability in big tournaments before; I played well in the last Grand Slam when the pressure was on. Coaches tell me I have talent and a lot of potential."

Just those few truths helped to release some tension and rebalance her approach so we could have a productive discussion about her upcoming match. The next day she played to win rather than not to lose and performed the best she had in months! She lost that match, but not because of poor self-talk—accepting her accomplishments neutralized the negative scenarios that she so easily fabricated in moments of stress. Sticking to the facts renewed her energy and resolve to stay focused on competing hard.

Facts lists can include any evidence or data about you on or off "the court." Results, specific statistics, hitting your sales or budget numbers, good performances, great plays, awards, feedback from others including bosses or coaches, media reviews, improvements, family support, academic grades—anything that is true and pleases you to note about yourself. This is a fun and elevating exercise!

When making your list, it's important to categorize your facts correctly. If you purposefully downplay your achievements or perpetuate inaccuracies about your performance life you will destroy your opportunities to perform better. Nothing and nobody is perfect, so do not insist that for a "fact" to make your list it must be a remarkably superior achievement. Be vigilant against mis-categorizing improvements as failures because either you or the outcome was not perfect. And don't discount an achievement because you wonder if it is repeatable—it *is* repeatable as you have done it at least once before.

An opera singer called my office looking for help. She wanted to address her mental toughness to move to the next level in her career as a soprano. She worried that things wouldn't go her way, and worried even more when they didn't, which left little room for things *to* go her way! She was right about the mental side of her performing—she needed to learn how to cope better.

During our first meeting I asked her about her proficiencies as a singer and a person. She seemed confused by the question, as if having strengths was beyond her. She went directly to where she was comfortable: rattling off her perceived failures and limitations with ease.

"I have very little confidence" (which was okay with me because, as discussed in chapter 4, confidence is overrated), "I got picked on in school, which made me feel different and on the outside of things—I still feel on the outside. At a young age I was told I was the whole package, but I didn't have any technique. I haven't been accepted to music programs for anything other than chorus work. I constantly audition but I am not getting even a small part. I give up when I lose my focus. I have a negative self-image, especially physically, and I find it hard to motivate myself even if it is something I will enjoy."

She continued unabated: "I feel like I use my anxiety about performing well as an excuse for not practicing or auditioning, which makes me feel worse. I find it very difficult to look at myself positively, and I tend to think I am never good enough and don't know how to change that."

This was supposed to be a list of her accomplishments! But this sometimes happens and I wasn't surprised by her comments, as many people let an unbalanced mindset overpower their approach to challenges and life. I was pleased that she was in my office as that meant she was ready for a change, and she needed to change what she said to herself, her inner voice.

When people have especially poor self-talk, when they are stubbornly negative and resistant to compliments, it can be a challenge to get started on their facts. My soprano was doing this very thing. She was hiding from herself. So, I pushed. I specifically asked her what gigs she had landed, what comments others had made regarding her talent or performances, and what personal characteristics she may even appreciate about herself. This was her homework. I gave her the week to settle, be honest, and look again. I wanted the full list, not just the easy, self-depreciating stuff that may or may not be true.

What she came back with was night-and-day different: "I am very passionate about what I love and I love singing. I have not given up on my singing even though I have wanted to many times. My singing teacher (a Metropolitan Opera alumnus) is still with me and helping me even though I am not the best student at times. I was told I have great stage presence. I am intuitive and try hard to follow my gut instincts because they are usually right. My piano teacher told my mom when I was a little girl that if I didn't have so much musical talent she would have suggested I quit music because I was never working at it." (This reminded her that she always had real talent, and that now she was finally doing something about it, which I thought was great.) "I have been told by quite a few people that I am the whole package. I am tall and fairly attractive. I am a kind and good person, I try to be helpful and caring to others, I am friendly and loyal. When I was younger, I was invited to Europe to train with a world-famous opera singer."

Her list was excellent. It was honest, not glossed over with useless affirmations. It showed her the good stuff that she had, over time, vigorously ignored. Her list even highlighted the need to keep being a better student (which she was already doing simply by coming to my office). I smiled and said, "Oh, so the person you are describing on this page isn't so bad, I guess?" "I guess not," she replied. "It was hard to do but it has helped me settle down about moving forward. Oh, and I have decided to go to an audition this week." This time her performance took her past the chorus and she snagged three solos in the production. She still had to mentally prepare for the weeks of rehearsals to come but was proud that she had not retreated from the initial challenge of auditioning. She could now see at least the possibility of further success.

Celebrating your successes (even quietly) will not make you complacent! Your fact list will not lessen your drive. You will not become cocky and overly content with yourself unless you already are a puffed-up and self-satisfied individual. And if you are, please settle, redo your fact list, and be honest this time. Being rightfully satisfied is not the same as being unwarrantedly satisfied. When done honestly, your fact list will help reduce your tension and keep you positively realistic about your capabilities and what is to come. Don't let the fear of becoming complacent stop you; look to your proof instead.

Review your list as often as you like—daily is not too much. Refer to it leading up to and including the day of your event, multiple times if you like, and even during the event itself if it will help keep you on track. One client mentioned in the weeks leading up to an important international competition that she started to go over her facts every morning and night and revisited the list casually during the day. She felt much clearer minded as a result and played better than she ever had. In fact, she made history as the best female in her country to ever play the game. Taking note of the good is critical to generating a constructive voice in your head.

Listing and reviewing your facts is just one part of good self-talk. Sustain your facts-based clear voice with the addition of smart talk. Smart talk is directive and takes you one step further. It guides you through tough situations. It reminds you of your cues and your *do*. It neutralizes harmful ideas and promotes effort and resolve. It supports calm and sharpens focus, it challenges and encourages, it is constructive and productive. Smart talk moves you forward in the moment.

Even a simple message has power. A mother volunteering on a school whitewater kayak trip made us both laugh when she recounted how she started her reluctant trip down a set of rapids hollering, "I CAN DO THIS! I CAN DO THIS! I CAN DO THIS!" By the time she got to the last rapid she was still repeating it, but much softer. Her on-the-spot and continuous commentary kept her engaged in the task of staying on top of the water and helped her to gradually calm down and gain control. She was proud of it, and rightly so!

Does your smart talk have to be positive? No, it doesn't. Positive talk can be overreaching and misleading. If a Formula 1 driver continually tells himself on race day "This is my day, I can win this race," yet consistently finishes at the back of the pack, he needs to adjust his talk. Of course, anything is possible, but telling yourself that you are the best when you clearly are not compromises your ability to improve. Unwarranted "positivity" can be discouraging and demoralizing over time, especially if it's used to avoid the anticipation of defeat or hide from the real work needed to become competitive. Positive talk is always welcome but to be effective it must be realistic.

Conversely, some negative talk can be surprisingly useful. A few negative thoughts during your day are to be expected: "I am not very good at speaking my mind," "I am not sure this will go my way," "I am nervous about this upcoming event and how I will do," "What if I'm not good enough?" Such comments may be negative but if accurate they are worthy of attention so you can adjust them. Rather than, "I really hope she doesn't beat me today," try, "She will beat me if I don't get my head in my game. I must be a little distracted and tense so slow down, take a breath or two, and pick a cue to focus on." Smart talk can be neutral and constructive. Just because it's not positive doesn't mean it is forbidden.

Negative talk is undermining when it is consistently inaccurate: "I am no good," "I never get it right, no wonder no one listens to me," "I don't deserve to be here," etc. People default to a negative mindset because it is easy. It allows them to stay passive and alleviates the discomfort of facing a challenge.

Choosing negativity absolves you from acting, protecting your vulnerability when reaching for your upper limits. In this psychological space you are safe. You can tell yourself that if you had really put your mind to it or worked harder or wanted it more you could have done it, that you still have the potential to win. Accepting failure before you perform hurts less than trying to succeed and coming up short. This negative talk prepares you to hold back and lets you off the hook from trying. And it needs to change.

Take stock of what you say to yourself and make sure it is smart talk. Try writing down the things you tend to say to yourself before, during, or after performing. Keep the top five good ones and change the others, then add more so you have new options. Make them positive (not delusional) or neutral (not negative). Simply put, if you don't believe what you are saying, don't say it. If you do believe what you say and it is harmful, rework it to make it constructive.

After qualifying a distant last in his division for a national Strongman competition, my new client had already accepted that he may not do well at all. He was anxious and his self-talk was crushing him: *Am I going to be embarrassingly bad? Am I a fraud? I may drop the sandbag on my head, I nearly did that once. Don't f—it up. I know I will let everyone down.* He was clearly getting in his own way.

Three months later, after some good work, he had a different mental approach to the competition. His alternative smart talk included: *I have prepared really well (mentally and physically). I can't escape when I'm onstage so I gotta go for it. My strength is there, I have improved a ton, I am way better when I breathe and stick to my cues. I feel strong enough to do this. Keep the bar close to my shins. Push straight up. This event is just sixty seconds long.* These points are positive but realistic, and where there was a negative he turned it into something constructive to do in the moment.

The day before the competition he said, "I feel ready to go," and he meant it. He kept a printout of his smart talk in his bag and looked at it before each event. At the end, he achieved several personal bests and earned a national record. His ability to improve had always been there, he just needed to coach himself to it.

Talk yourself through your performance. Tell yourself what to do, when to do it, and what to be ready for.

I was invited to join a teambuilding day with the scouts and management of a Major League Baseball team I worked for. Formula 1 kart racing sounded like a fun change from the typical paintball or pool hall get-togethers I experienced with other teams.

Once all of us wannabe drivers were lined up at the start, complete with racing suits and personalized helmets, the trash-talking was at full blast. By the fourth and final race I had figured out how not to flip the go-kart so I decided to go for it. I knew I would need to talk my way through the entire race to keep pushing forward, to go as fast as I could every lap. I started off directing myself with my calm inner voice but ended up literally yelling into my helmet. I was barking at myself to HOLD the wheel tight around the entire turn, or get OFF the brakes NOW and hit the throttle HARD, or BREATHE on the straightaways, or just GO, GO, GO!

I knew if I didn't keep connected to what I needed to do on the track (or when one of the guys blocked or bumped me) I would end up distracted, slow down, and lose position. Afterward, a young scout bitterly complained when my name popped up at the top of the leaderboard. He didn't know that talking myself through the race kept me pushing through, and right past him.

Use your facts and your smart talk often. Have them written down and ready to go. And if you need to, use your outside voice as well as your inside voice. One of my beach volleyball players learned in the world championship final that she needed to talk to herself out loud. Only then did her comments become real to her and impossible to ignore. Now in warm-up or mid-match, she will *talk* and she doesn't care if others hear because it keeps her playing some of the best beach volleyball in the world. Besides, she says, "We are much better if we are talking and yelling and cheering and animated, so facts and smart talk fit right into our best game planning!"

Smart talk is such an effective and simple strategy, but it requires honesty first. Remember that coming up with your self-talk has two elements. First, make your facts list to highlight your truths and your proofs to get you in the right frame of mind. Then make your short list of constructive smart talk reminders to use in the moment, in the hours leading up to your big performance, or every day generally.

Our five performers enjoyed formulating their facts and tweaking their smart talk to help them be their best in the high-pressure moments they knew were coming.

Riley

Riley had never thought of making a facts list before but liked what he saw once he got into it:

*   I was drafted high.
*   My face-off stats are excellent.
*   I prepared very well in the off-season and my conditioning is the best it has ever been.
*   I'm an experienced pro of five years.
*   My general manager told me that the team doesn't have many guys like me as I am big, strong, and smart on the ice.
*   I am proud of my university degree.

Do all the facts have to be about your specific performance concerns? No, not at all! Riley was proud of his postsecondary education, even though it had nothing to do with hockey. But thinking about it reminded him he has achieved a lot. As an alternative to his usual self-doubting smart talk, Riley made sure to create a list he could rely on, one that was positive. He also incorporated some of his cues because good smart talk will often lead you to your *do*:

*   I can only control my game so focus on myself.
*   I'm great when I keep moving my feet.
*   Hold on to the puck and skate with it if you want to make things happen.

* I can compete with these guys, I've been doing it all sum-
mer in training.
* It is okay to be tense, it means I want to do well, so
breathe.
* I am good at this; I know what I am doing.
* Do my thing, it works!

Cameron

Cameron was a very modest person and never spoke of her achievements, so I pressed her. To get her started, I asked if she had any professional acknowledgments of note (both of us knowing full well she had several). That got her rolling:

* I got this promotion because I am good at my job,
the head of the school said I was the best candidate by far.
* At graduation I was acknowledged by the students as an
outstanding teacher.
* I consistently receive excellent performance reviews for my
teaching.
* My students are top achievers on standardized exams.
* My students ask for help when they have a problem, course
related or personal.
* I interact well with people I know, I listen well.
* I have become a killer pickleball player and recently won a
medal at a tournament.

Cameron felt grounded and poised when she thought about her facts—that's the point. Now she felt she needed only a few smart talk statements to help keep her on track in the moment:

* Stay calm, I have what it takes.
* I'm here for a good reason, my boss believes
  in me.
* I'm actually good at this, people respond well to me,
  they like me.

Ty

Ty had many achievements, and listing them came easily:

* I play in the NFL and I love it!
* I'm good at reading the field.
* My teammates and I work well together.
* I have a really strong arm.
* I get paid a lot and am very grateful for my job.
* I have a conference championship ring.
* I am tough, I don't complain.
* I have a fabulous wife.
* I am very involved in my charity and we have been
  highly successful at raising money.

Ty's self-talk was naturally positive, but he wanted to focus on preparing to handle conflict well in the future with good smart talk:

* Stand up for myself.
* Stay calm, don't back down if I get pushback.
* My opinion here is important, speak up.
* Decide how I want to play and do it.
* Say why it's not working and what could work
  better.

Alex

While at a tournament with Alex, I asked her for her facts. Like many people she was initially reluctant to share (for fear of showing conceit or wishing to avoid ridicule), but once I asked about her world ranking she relaxed. She understood we were talking about objective truths and not delving into the emotionally fraught territory of hopes, wants, and potential falsehoods. Which is precisely why facts are helpful. She called them her "fun facts" and would sarcastically recite her top three (with a huge eye roll) when I would ask. But she did it:

* I am ranked in the top fifty in the world.
* I've won indoor and outdoor junior nationals.
* I've been a high-performance player since I was ten years old.
* I am on track for a professional career.
* I'm fit, strong, and athletic.
* I've beaten top players.
* I have an excellent, consistent serve.
* I do a lot of volunteer work, which I like.
* I have a 90 percent average at school.
* I am being recruited by good universities.

She followed up her "fun facts" with some great smart talk:

* I've done this before, I can do it.
* Be hard to play against.
* Stick to my game plan.
* Encourage myself: "Come on!"
* Make my opponent play the extra shot.
* Play one point at a time.

Jamie

Jamie was an accomplished individual and felt better about himself after listing his facts:

* I earned my MBA, I guess I am intelligent enough.
* I have a great job and am progressing well.
* I'm making a good living.
* I work hard.
* My numbers this year are very strong.
* I got great feedback on my last project.
* My boss gives me helpful evaluations.
* I'm creative, I write music, I play piano and guitar.
* I love to cook and am good at it.
* I'm good at my hobbies.
* I played sports in university.
* My parents are proud of me.
* My girlfriend loves me.

He had to consciously change the way he let himself derail his actions when he felt threatened or unsure, so he reworked his default destructive self-talk into focused smart talk:

* It's not me, it's not personal, let it pass.
* My boss is trying to help me with his comments, I know that.
* In the end it always works out and I always do a good job.
* Take a breath and slow down.
* Deal with yourself, be a good guy.
* Stay respectful.

———

Jamie was ready to start talking his way through his worries and his anger. He and the other four performers all had excellent self-talk to use before or during their big performances. Now it was time to practice with a little daydreaming.

Chapter Fifteen

Skill 4:
Keep Daydreaming

We all watch images play out in our minds. Whether reminiscing, regretting moments from the past, planning the future, or getting lost in impossible heroics and improbable catastrophes, our imagination is engaged more often than we realize. Why not use it to prepare for pressure moments?

Focused daydreaming lets you create new experiences and re-create productive ones from your past with an eye to help you minimize errors, improve abilities, and get results. Recently at the US Open, an iconic tennis legend told me that much of her success was due to mental practice, to mental movement without overt physical movement. "It was all about imagining and daydreaming for me, I did it all the time. I mentally rehearsed everything." Daydreaming with a purpose does not get enough credit for how it can quickly help you settle, plan good things, and pull you toward a desired outcome.

Mental practice isn't only seeing a picture in your mind; it involves all your senses. If you imagine yourself on a beach, you may see white sand and palm trees, or smooth stones and an old-growth forest, depending on your vantage point. You may also have a sense of smelling salt water, coconut sunblock, or crisp air. You might hear gently rolling waves or a pounding surf, feel your feet in the sand or the rain on your skin. You can choose which senses to use and how many to include, any combination that helps you inhabit the scene you are creating. Musicians may hear more, chefs may taste more, and athletes may feel more, all while seeing it too. In this virtual space, you can control the action and the outcome.

Daydreaming constructively will help you learn a new skill or maintain an already competent one. It can motivate you to act in a situation rather than hesitate, to reduce stress and shift your mood, to reunite with your highlights, to familiarize, to prepare for a tough conversation, to plan your next attack, even to enhance your body's healing from an injury (research and scholarly study in this area is well established). A business executive and owner of various professional sports teams explained to me that when doing business, his mental practice is like playing chess. When negotiating deals, he plans every potential move. He constantly thinks about each possible scenario, the next move, the countermove, and then the next three moves. He thinks each option out to the very end. He may not win every detail of every deal to his total satisfaction, but he always has a solution at the ready and is never caught off guard by his opponents' tactics. The applications of mental practice are immense!

Mental practice has repeatedly been shown to enhance performance in any field. In my early career I was a hospital-based researcher in psychiatry. Now as a consulting performance psychologist, I am still involved in medical research, most recently with surgeons looking at how mental practice affects stress, surgical skills, and performance. In an initial study I did with the University of Toronto we found that the group of residents who had mental practice training (in addition to their technical instruction) performed better, even in a crisis scenario, than the group that received only technical instruction. We were pretty excited about these results and are continuing to look at mental practice in our follow-up study as it may be an innovative, practical, and cost-effective way to improve training of surgeons and ultimately patient care and safety.

How does mental practice work to improve performance? Our thoughts can absolutely influence our bodies and emotions. Think of a perfect, bright-yellow lemon. Take a moment to see yourself cutting it into wedges. Take a juicy piece in your hand and smell it. Now take a big bite. Did you pucker a little or salivate slightly? That physiological response lets you know that your mind and body are connected.

Imagine walking into a meeting and unexpectedly being asked to stand up and speak to the group on an unfamiliar topic. For some, this situation will immediately raise their blood pressure and heart rate or give them an unwelcome shot of stress hormones. Whether you are imagining this scenario or actually experiencing it, the same parts of the brain are being activated.

A ten-meter platform diver mentally rehearsing a reverse dive with four somersaults (very difficult!) will neurologically fire the same muscles he would when actually doing the dive physically, but at a much lower level. Imagined actions are perceived by the body as if they were real. The better you can control your mental imagery, the better you will be able to execute in the performance environment. If you want to gain results, even by a smidge, "see" it before you go live.

What if you think you can't? Emerson was starting a salon business and was feeling overwhelmed by all the things that could go wrong (but hadn't yet). "I know imagery could help me more fully picture and design the details of the space I want to create and the customer experience I want to provide, but imagery has never worked for me. I just can't do it. I can't see anything clearly in my head."

I hear this a lot so I asked some questions to spur things on. "What color is your bedroom painted? Where is your bed in the room? What other furniture do you see? What is on the walls?" She answered easily. "Now stand outside the room and put your hand on the door handle, push the door open and step inside. Go sit on your bed." She did. Emerson could certainly use her imagination; she just needed to take her time and start with something familiar and concrete.

I then asked her to take a full minute of slow, easy breaths (which is about six if you are truly relaxing) and sink farther into the cushy chair she was sitting in. "Now tell me about the fantastic design you are planning for your salon." She did that too, in wonderful detail. A little direction and she was on her way. Many people say they can't imagine a new, never-before-experienced scenario, but typically that is just tension in the way. Rather than fight through the murky, rushed, and disjointed images that flit past their eyes, people assume they can't envision. Knowing to slow yourself before you try makes all the difference. Take your time, then create.

Meditating for an hour every morning is pleasing to some (and if this is you, keep it up!), but for performing I favor the kind of mental practice that is brief, frequent, and targets specific actions. I sort the types of practice into five categories to make it easy to know what to daydream about. These are chill, skill, highlight, fight-back, and step-it-up imagery.

Chill is about practicing becoming calm, staying cool, or remaining composed in any situation. This could take your mind to the beach of your choice, a beautiful room, sitting with your dog, or anyplace that you like (or would like) to forest bathe, meadow walk, or mountain gaze. Chill daydreaming can take you anywhere you want to go, so go where you can feel loose and watch your calm unfold. It is about slowing your breathing and inviting yourself to relax. You can do this willingly simply because it feels good. But it keeps your tension down and can settle you before anything stressful, like having your blood pressure taken, after an uncomfortable interaction (or in anticipation of one), before an exam, or between shots on the golf course.

Skill imagery allows you to try a new technique or strategy, to rehearse a task you are already capable of, to plan a performance or an interaction, or familiarize yourself with a venue or protocol. An NBA client wanted to start the season well but was disappointed with his shooting after the first week. Giving up easy layups was derailing him, and he wanted to quickly extinguish the problem. After evaluating, he realized he was distracted by the defender barreling down on him and he wasn't finishing his shot. It was a simple fix. He did some daydreaming and each time saw himself push off his leg powerfully, look for the rim, and extend his hand high to the rim or backboard, scoring every time. He used daydreaming to reconnect to properly executing the shot. He incorporated this layup *clip* into his pregame warm-up and while on the bench during the game. He made improvements immediately.

Highlight imagery connects you to your favorite personal accomplishments, much like your facts list, but with more attention to the details of your victories. Reviewing your smooth chip shots, your top times, the compliments you have received, or the kindnesses you are known for keeps you closer to your abilities and less susceptible to anxious negativity. See your successes and re-create them in your mind often. One client looked at some video from his recent Olympics and said, "I can't believe I was that good." He was truly surprised at his performances; he had forgotten what he could do. He decided on the spot to daydream more about the good stuff.

Fight-back imagery is often overlooked but learning to quickly come back from mistakes or fussy reactions is a mega weapon when trying to be better next time. This imagery will help you push back on challenges or face your hot spots, and it's great for mentally practicing the things you aren't good at. *See* yourself outlasting your opponent when you don't think you have much left, or turning back and chasing down that ball or puck your opponent just took from you. An equestrian client used this type of imagery to literally get back on his horse after a serious injury. An accidental kick in the face left him with a broken jaw and short a few teeth. On his first few rides back, he was tentative when his horse felt unsettled under him or when he bucked a little. My rider began to practice *seeing* himself ride his big, beautiful horse "forward" whenever he felt uncomfortable. He saw himself sit tall, open his chest, sit in the middle of the saddle, and put his "leg on" to move the horse from agitation (perceived or real) to moving with purpose. He was back in the saddle in no time.

Step-it-up imagery encourages you to do just that. Be bold, change your script, risk envisioning something bigger than or different from your status quo, create new outcomes. Make it up and go big! Get comfortable with what could be new and real for you. That same tennis legend I mentioned above also told me that in her mind she used to "chase down impossible shots," not to fantasize beyond reality but to innovate how she might do it and push her limits.

When do you do it? It's easy. Take five seconds in the shower to *see* yourself in that power outfit you feel good in as you walk into that meeting. While you are waiting for your toast to pop up, *see* yourself toss the ball high and use your legs when you serve today at the tennis club. Before you putt, take a moment to *see* the line you will take to the hole. When preparing to audition a new piece of music, *see* your fingers hitting the center of the keys. Before making a phone call that you are nervous about, take ten or fifteen seconds to connect to your calm, slower voice; maybe sit (you can lie down too) comfortably for five minutes and *see* yourself hitting the key points of your speech with the right inflection and emphasis.

One IndyCar driver I know would daydream once he was securely strapped into his race car waiting for the "Gentlemen, start your engines" command. He would run through a couple of quick daydreams, seeing himself being calm and getting a clean start when the green flag was waved (not easy when you are only two inches away from other cars), or handling the car expertly through a treacherous corner.

This is focused daydreaming at its finest! It is informal and you can do it on the fly, anywhere at any time. The content can be planned or not. It can be done in short bursts that you can infuse frequently into your day. It can't hurt you, it can only help. And it is that easy. You can close your eyes or keep them partly open. You can roll through your images as if you are watching yourself on video—try to see yourself from different views and angles. Or see yourself from behind your own eyes as you would when you are executing in real time. This inside view lets you more easily connect to the physical movement of the real action. So when hitting a forehand you would see your hands and racquet out in front of you as you hit up on the ball and feel the racquet accelerate through it. Use either or both views, in real time, slow motion, or even fast-forward—just make sure you see something! Practice producing a clear, bright picture and work to control the movement within your view.

If you have trouble getting a vivid image that you can manipulate as you wish, remember to do a breathing exercise or a chill daydream first before you try to paint a masterpiece. Once you settle, try it again. Start small, then add moving parts.

How long does it take? Literally seconds. A single clip lasting from five seconds to a full minute works well. How often should you practice? If you spent thirty seconds in a quality daydream four times a day, that is a whole two minutes of mental practice a day. The benefits accrue with frequency rather than total time spent, so a good target is practicing several days of the week.

You can do more if you want but I don't think it is necessary. That said, during the weeks and days leading up to an event, feel free to increase your practice as it will add to your preparation, both mental and technical.

Depending on the importance of and your proficiency with an upcoming task, adjust your practice to your comfort level. You can think through the performance from start to finish or focus on a specific part or different sections of the event that need work. Be sure to practice for stressful and unexpected situations; see yourself in the moment or in situ. You don't want to arrive to find eleven interviewers around a huge conference table instead of the one you planned for (this happened to me once and it was a rough start). Similarly, don't let a surprise derail you, like a critical comment, or a technical problem with your slideshow.

Daydreaming in short bursts, regularly during the day and consistently over the week, is an easy and enjoyable way to advance your preparation and your performance. Our daydreaming can be self-directed, constant, and creative, so use it to your advantage.

Mental practice can also be more formal and guided. The surgeons in our mental practice group mentioned above were given a mental practice script detailing each step of the operation they were to learn and perform. A voiceover of the script emphasized important cues to *feel* and *see* at each step of the operation. They rehearsed with the script and also engaged in their own focused mental practice or daydreaming at their convenience during the day.

Receiving assistance from a script or an audio recording or video (or a combination) can be a relaxed way to learn a task, a behavior, or facilitate the connection between your mind and body. One of my clients always went straight to YouTube to review the operation she was preparing for the next day, while another watched onboard video (video of a race captured from the driver's viewpoint) to familiarize himself with the racetrack he would compete on the next week.

Guided scripts are plentiful and easily accessible online. There are scripts specially designed for relaxation, for anything as varied as people recovering from knee reconstruction surgery or for being more kind to yourself. Some exercises last for a couple of minutes, others up to an hour. You can even write and record a script yourself detailing how you want to perform.

Guided practice can be a good place to start if you are unfamiliar with the task or have trouble relaxing. Letting a voice take you to a beautiful place is a great way to lessen stress, but you don't always have time to lie down and hit the play button. So, rehearse purposefully on your own and often. Be ready to quickly connect to your imagination right before you step on the stage, walk into that intimidating cocktail reception, or sit and regroup between shifts during your hockey game.

Use the types of imagery that suit you best or that you enjoy the most. As daydreaming is so easy to practice and generates immediate benefits, you can try what you feel will fit the moment or suit your mood. You already daydream naturally so take the opportunity to expand your repertoire to include scenarios and outcomes you may not have previously considered. You can use all five types of daydreaming, just one, or any combination you prefer. But open yourself to purposeful daydreaming in some capacity, at the very least investing in some chill daydreaming here and there.

Be easy on yourself when your mind wanders during practice. It's no biggie, just gently bring your focus back to the scene in front of you and carry on. Our performers selected the daydreams that worked best for them and knew they could adjust their options at any time.

Riley

As a pro athlete, Riley was accustomed to watching video of himself, alone or with a coach, so daydreaming with purpose came easily to him.

Chill: Riley thought about his great girlfriend and liked to see himself hanging out with her and their dog.

Skill: To ease his transition from summer preparation to his team's training camp, Riley began to familiarize himself with the intensity he would feel when he stepped on the ice in front of his teammates and coaches. He would *see* himself warming up for practice fully dressed in his team gear, stick in hand, skating smoothly and powerfully with the other players. He also saw himself in scrimmages shooting to the top corners of the net and stopping in front of the net rather than skating by it.

Highlight: He reviewed a video compilation of his stronger plays and then replayed them in his head here and there during the day.

Fight-back: When he saw a mistake in any of his daydreams, he did not stop the clip and restart it; he fought through the image and saw himself make a great recovery, even if it seemed unrealistic. Sometimes he would slow the image down to make it easier to correct the error and then continue the daydream at normal speed.

Cameron

Cameron had never thought about mentally practicing anything; usually what floated through her mind organically centered on what could go wrong. She liked the idea of having a script as she felt more in control of the uncertainty she tended to feel.

Chill: Cameron felt positive and peaceful when she daydreamed about sitting by herself curled up in a comfy chair reading a great novel.

Skill: She liked to practice seeing herself composed, standing tall, smiling and chatting easily in business and personal interactions.

Highlight: She reviewed a previous alumni event where she felt she performed well (she rated her performance a 7 out of 10) and zoomed in on the warm and welcome way people had responded to her.

Step-it-up: In an effort to change her default tendency to avoid new and unfamiliar social situations, Cameron continued to refine her behavior by seeing herself approach strangers at functions and speaking to groups with charm, wit, and ease. She wasn't sure she would ever accomplish the wit part, but she was certainly advancing her charm and ease.

Ty

As a naturally easygoing person, but still very driven, Ty took to daydreaming with enthusiasm.

Chill: Ty liked to fish, anywhere and for anything. For a restful mental retreat he would see himself spending a lazy day fishing back home.

Skill: Ty saw himself walking down the hall to any big meeting (or media interview) loose and relaxed. He practiced seeing himself enter the conversation from a good place, open and inviting.

Fight-back: He imagined the worst reaction he could get from his coach (loud, dismissive, and critical) and how he would handle it. He saw himself go to his step-it-up daydreaming to be ready for this real possibility.

Step-it-up: Ty would see himself making a decision on how he thought they should run some specific plays. He'd push back by speaking up and finishing his thoughts, but always calmly, keeping his tone of voice down and shoulders relaxed. In his head he'd ask for input, making it a collaborative process.

Alex

As a dynamic and highly competitive player, Alex had a lot of positives to daydream about, but also parts of her game she wanted to improve. She used all five daydreaming techniques.

Chill: When I asked Alex if she used any chill imagery, she said, "I don't do that. Maybe I should but nothing comes to mind. But I like to Breathe It Out a lot." I thought that was an excellent option, so Alex started to visualize herself breathing it out and that became her chill imagery.

Skill: Alex loved to daydream about her shots and tactics and picture herself on the specific court she would play on in competition. She paid particular attention to the areas of her game she considered to be weaker: her backhand, her overhead volley, and going to the net (she needed to go more). She would run these clips from behind her eyes, and from an aerial view too. She would even see how her opponent would likely return her ball and then play a great countershot.

Highlight: Alex liked to have fun seeing her great serve and her big powerful forehand emphasizing a fast finish to the shot.

Fight-back: Alex tended to flounce and fuss around the court when things weren't going her way. She would look beseechingly at her coach sitting in the stands as if he should or could do something to immediately fix her diminishing results. This giant breach of self-agency robbed her of her usual performance power, sending her into a flurry of unnecessary errors. To practice shifting from this drifting, she pictured herself standing tall, turning and walking slowly toward the back wall of the court (to take her focus off her opponent), shaking out her shoulders and arms, then walking purposefully back to the baseline and using her legs to serve or keeping her feet moving if she was to receive. As a release and to be realistic, she sometimes allowed herself to look super exasperated but only until the next play. Alex challenged herself to get her head back together after two errors as opposed to four or five.

Step-it-up: Seeing herself play loose and with tactical precision against higher-ranked opponents.

Jamie

The best way for Jamie to make a meaningful change was to practice calmness when there was no pressure.

Chill: Before meetings with his boss, Jamie would take a three-to-five-minute mental vacation. He used one of his apps to listen to a guided meditation on mindful walking or watch peaceful imagery of clouds, water, or the night sky. This helped him connect to his mind so he could remember to ease any growing tension. The guided exercises were teaching him to re-create these feelings on his own.

Skill: When he felt criticized, he'd see himself being quiet, breathing slower, closing his mouth, listening longer (and then a little longer), and accepting what was being said.

Fight-back: When he'd falter, Jamie would decide to fight through it. He'd see his lack of self-control (yelling, whining, inciting, blaming, excusing) and then shut up, say nothing. Not a word. If he was struggling to contain his behavior, he'd see himself walk away.

Step-it-up: Jamie extended his skill imagery by envisioning a relaxed, respectful, reliable, understanding, and empathic self in his pressure situations. He'd see himself being this man so he could become this man.

Jamie's step-it-up daydream shows why this skill is so important. If we can't imagine what we wish to be—if we don't honestly try to fully articulate it to ourselves—how will we ever achieve it?

———

At this point, our performers have gone through the first two steps of the process and all four skills, listing their hot spots and strategies for addressing them. Taken all together, these points are a master plan for successfully performing under pressure. But there's still one step left to further refine the plan and ensure you stick to it.

Chapter Sixteen

Stick to the Plan

In the previous chapters we've seen how to plan your performances so you can dial into what will make you great. Now it's time to make that plan and learn how to stick to it. In this final step of the performance process, we will pull it all together to simplify and consolidate your skills and strategies into a go-to solution that you can shift to in the moment. Your plan is a force field between you and a poor performance. Protect yourself from super derailers and other distractions by having one ready to go. Even the greatest performers need this.

Robyn was ripping through each round as though Wimbledon were for kids. She played the match of her life in the semifinals, not missing a single ball. Like everyone else, Robyn was surprised to have played her way past one of the perennial queens of the professional circuit right into her first Grand Slam final. Better yet, she had previously beaten the other finalist. Robyn was playing well and enjoying the ride. "I was so pleased to be in the final, I didn't think about winning it. The mistake I made was that I didn't have a plan." Without one, she lost.

Robyn was gratified with her performance, her big-time prize money, and her unexpected place in the history books. But three or four months later she was angry. "I could have won. I gave her too much credit. She didn't put me under a lot of pressure, and I was too gentle on her. I should have been more aggressive on some shots, and I didn't think about my tactics enough. I should have been ready to fight, to go to the net more, to play her backhand, to get to the ball, to serve harder, to pick up the intensity of the match, to try something and everything. I lost my chance." Robyn is now a fantastic coach and tells her players: "Don't lose your chance. Have a plan and don't back off."

What does a good plan look like? Short and structured. Your master plan (chapters 12 through 15) will contain around a dozen relevant reminders and cues. Do you need all those strategies every time you perform? No. That much thinking will splinter your performance. The trick is to select those few strategies you need to execute *in the moment*. Focus on the areas of your performance that are not automatic, on the actions you want to improve, make more consistent, or not forget about. I break performance plans into three sections (and only three): your warm-up, during the event, and your #1 focus for the event. Each section contains your most salient strategies.

What do you need to warm up well? Anything that relaxes you or reminds you of your cues. You can pull your strategies from any skill zone you like. Some people remind themselves to stretch more, run through a breathing exercise, and do a couple of quick daydreams about a technique or desirable state of mind. Three bullet points are enough to keep you engaged and mindful, but you can add one or two more if you want since during a warm-up you have the time to get settled before you perform.

What do you need to do during the event? Drill down to those strategies that are critical to your execution; usually performance cues are best here. You may have six in your master plan but select your best one or two for your go-to plan. Also select a strategy or two for when you have a break in the action, such as between shifts, games or sets, races, pieces, songs, runs, phone calls, questions, or steps in a procedure. It's helpful to have that extra strategy to keep you focused during downtime.

Finish off your plan by making sure you extract a #1 focus from your master plan. This is the one thing that you know if you *do* out there, you can pull it together quickly and keep yourself on track. If you freeze or get foggy you can always go to this one reminder to get back into your rhythm. It is the technique or tactic to grab on to in a panic or free fall. When you are about to give up and hit the eject button out of the task, hit this reset button instead. This will give you the chance to settle and resume your focus. Mistakes will happen, as will serendipitous excellence, and both can be distracting. So be ready with this contingency to regroup in the moment. The best contingencies center around breathing (taking a couple of slower breaths as in Breathe It Out) or having one cue to do: breathe on the way to your towel box, get your feet moving, speak louder, take smaller steps, etc. Just pick one.

One client's plans were beautifully laid out on an iPad in bullet form with precise headings for each part of the racecourse. I loved the thought and design that went into it, but it was too much. His content was great and accurate but far too detailed to be accessible in the moment when things were moving so quickly, mentally and physically. We would good-naturedly battle over what could stay and what had to go. We eventually got it down from an entire page to just the three sections. Only the critical reminders made the cut. This clarity and structure helped calm his stress level and direct his focus during the competition. And his results got better. When a plan is too detailed it distracts from one's real performance needs and becomes a derailer itself.

It's important to prepare a plan for each performance, or at least the big ones. It takes only minutes and clarifies your approach to the task. You can create a plan for an upcoming game and then reuse it the following week or make adjustments depending on your needs. Public speakers may want to keep their plan in a drawer, ready to be pulled out and reviewed when it is time to present again. Or a skier may adjust parts of their plan slightly for every run, depending on what is working or the terrain to be navigated. Even if you don't change your plan, take a moment to rewrite it as it will help refresh your performance intentions. Writing out your bullet points will help your retention in the moment.

Avoid making changes for variety or to tinker. Rather, change your plan based on what you want to focus on. The idea is to keep refining your actions as you get better or to get better if the last plan didn't work as well as you'd hoped. Remember, it's a process.

Finlay and I were texting before a big downhill skiing event. He had finished his master plan. He knew his super derailers well: worrying about how I am feeling (confidence) and forgetting to think about the skiing stuff, focusing too much on results, getting distracted by other racers talking in the lodge and at the start, and getting a bad start. He had over twenty strategies and reminders to choose from to create a go-to plan. It was time to write it down for the race.

The only paper he could find in the chalet was a Post-it Note pad. "Perfect!" I wrote. "Make your plan fit on one Post-it Note and send a photo." He sent me a great plan but on two pages. I texted back: "Too long. Please rewrite and fit it all on one note page, without miniature writing." His next version was crammed but he did it!

Over the next few race weekends his plans got shorter and more concise. He adjusted his second section (during the race) to incorporate a specific part he needed to work on, a cue to ensure he had a good start. For the rest of the season he wrote a plan for each race and sent me a photo. We would discuss if needed, but mostly it was for him to keep up this helpful habit.

He kept planning and kept getting better results. His mind was sharpened and he could stay connected to the course by sticking to his cues. His mental warm-up helped him settle and get ready to explode out of the start and carry his focus from gate to gate with fewer gaps in attention. If he could stay focused for increasingly more gates down the course, he would ski faster and finish better. He started the season with low expectations and finished it by qualifying for the world championships. Now he is a big planner, but keeps it to a Post-It Note.

Some of us need to keep our reminders in hand, literally. A young excitable player on an NBA team that I worked with had trouble staying focused during games. Some days he was a dominant force in the game and on others you forgot he was even on the floor. While I was on a road trip with the team, he decided to confront his inconsistency. He wanted to learn how to plan his game.

Sitting together on the team bus from the hotel to the arena we did a speed version of a game plan for that night. He wrote it out, put the paper in his pocket, and was all set. That night he put together an outstanding first half. Soon into the third period he was not playing with the same purpose and was missing shots—he was drifting. When he was subbed out, he sat down on his chair with force and frustration. I was sitting in the row behind him and saw him suddenly start scrabbling around looking for something on the floor. He turned around and said, "Dana! Where is my plan! I can't find my plan!"

So off I went to the visitors' locker room to do my own scrabbling around looking for his paper. I finally found it among his belongings in his stall and then made my way back to my seat behind the players. I slipped the plan to him and he took a long look, adjusted his posture, sat back in his chair, and reminded himself of his *do*. His mind was always running fast but all he needed was a quick reminder *during* the game of what had been working for him so he could reset and finish the game the way he wanted to. He had to have his plan in hand for when he revved too high. He got good at keeping his little paper nearby.

You might be thinking, *I don't think I need a plan. I don't like to think about it too much. I know what to do so I like to just go out and do it.* If you really want to go this route, do your thing. But when I hear this from a client I always push back, at least once. No matter how good you are or how often you have done it, if the performance is meaningful or worth your effort, it behooves you to be ready to be good. Even taking one minute to think it through, to decide on a #1 focus—to consciously drop your shoulders or remind yourself to run through a quick daydream—can be enough to release tension or dial in on one thing that will keep you on track. Don't carelessly breeze by making a plan in order to avoid your feelings. Deal with the pressure you may feel to have a good result or avert a bad one by having an explicit plan ready to go, even if it is a mini plan. Finish the process and have something specific to grab on to mentally if you falter or if you need to elevate your game, especially when the game really counts.

Then the trick is to stick with it. Have you ever prepared well for a performance and been pleased with the result? Did you let this satisfaction carry you into the next performance without bothering with the same mental planning? And were you then dejected or surprised and wonder why you didn't perform with the same quality? When I hear, "I did well last time, I've got this," or, "Finally! I figured it out. I am good to go now," I am excited for the person, but I think *Not so fast* and gently suggest that we aren't done yet.

You shouldn't expect it all to happen again automatically. It is great when things go well so keep them going your way. And resist the urge to abandon your plan if things aren't going your way, or if you make a mistake. Sticking to it allows you to start strong or reset when you aren't happy.

Even established performers can refine their outcomes by strengthening their "stickiness." Another NBA client, a well-respected, versatile veteran took great care to plan his game, but when he missed two shots in a row he jettisoned his go-to plan. He didn't stick with what he knew worked best. He didn't tell himself to "stay smooth." He just admonished himself for the misses, which of course compounded his errors. He needed to stick to it and keep resetting rather than capitulate to regret about the last shot or uncertainty about the next one or worry about the media or his stats.

When we spoke I worked hard to convince him to redirect himself in the moment as I knew it was the best way for him to be in the strongest technical and mental position to get results. Also, it couldn't possibly hurt; it could only help his play. Once he made it work a couple of times in a game, he was stuck on sticking with it. He pulled his shooting back in line and had a very satisfying season. Ultimately, he loved the control he felt within himself and being able to put a whole game together regularly rather than only parts of one here and there.

How can you tell if your plan is working? Track your outcomes. Once your event is over do a brief evaluation. Do it the same day or the next so you don't lose the nuance of how you felt or what you did, but make sure to do it. This self-feedback helps you improve purposefully so give it serious contemplation.

How did you perform? Rate yourself on a scale of 1 (lousy) to 10 (brilliant). Resist unnecessary reproach or unearned leniency. This self-rating is about how you executed in the circumstances; it is not a measure of results only. You can work to control your actions but not always your results.

During a sales call you may have presented your products and services well but the potential client can't find the budget at that time. You may have played your round with poise and skill but missed the travel cut with your university team that week because others were even better that day. In both instances you didn't get the result you wanted but you performed well and maybe with excellence. In life you can play a great game but still lose.

Conversely, you could have been traded to yet another NHL team because you weren't committed to fitness or basic nutrition or to managing your on-ice assignments but end up on a strong team that wins the Stanley Cup at the end of the season. You could botch your big job interview but get the position anyway because others had turned the offer down. If you want to improve, rate performance over results.

With your honest 1–10 rating in place, ask yourself three questions: What did I do well? What didn't go so well? And what do I need to adjust for next time? If more structure will help you analyze your performance, start by checking in on your tension. Were you calm and loose or tense and tight? How was your mental warm-up—did you do any and if so was it good enough? How effective were your performance cues? Were they helpful, or were they perhaps not the right ones? How constructive was your smart talk and did you use your facts list? How effective was your daydreaming before the event or between sets (uncontrolled and vague or controlled and vivid)? How focused were you during the performance? Were you distracted by a hot spot or pushed off your game by a super derailer? In challenging situations, how well did you stick to the plan and refocus? The best responses get to the heart of the matter.

Watching an NFL game from the sidelines is grippingly compelling and wildly entertaining. There is a lot of movement, a lot of noise, a lot of emotion, and you have to be vigilant or you will get smoked by really big guys running out of bounds (I learned this after a few rather harrowing misses). It is also a fabulous place to get some work done.

After one game a player and I took advantage of the walk back to the locker room by chatting and doing a quick evaluation. He rated himself an 8 out of 10; he was rightfully pleased with how he had picked up the quality of his game compared to the previous weeks. He felt he "got off the ball" fast and stayed low to gain power and leverage when running "through" his opponents. Excellent work—he followed his top performance cues.

I then asked what didn't go so well and he wasn't immediately sure. People get stuck on this question so I asked my usual follow-ups: "What could you have done better? Where did your play break down, even just a little? During the plays that didn't work as well, what were you doing more of? Less of?" After a moment he said, "I could have finished some plays better. Usually, if I don't physically go through a player, I move around him fast. That is how I am disruptive on the field. On some plays today I didn't do that as often as I could have. To make more impact plays I need to throw players off me and step around them faster, not just tie them up. I can do more." His one adjustment for next week's game plan was to tell himself to "finish" the tackle. Then go sack the quarterback. This is what true self-evaluation looks like and is how real improvement happens.

Keep building your mental talent through planning and evaluating. The World Cup ski season is an international pressure-packed jaunt from one spectacular resort to another. A client was heading into the new season very well prepared and excited for the first race weekend. Except her last few days of training weren't going smoothly mentally. She was distracted. She was fast but wondering if she was fast enough. She was now vacillating between high expectations and reserved hopefulness. She had a clear race plan and knew she absolutely had to stick with it from start to finish.

I watched the live results online and was pleased for her as her results were elite. On our postrace debriefing call, she acknowledged her strong results but rated her performance low at 6 out of 10 (she is a hard marker). She knew something was holding her back. Her assessment revealed that she veered off her race plan. She forgot about her facts list before the race, in her warm-up, and glossed over her cues during the race. Overlooking her go-to strategies dulled her execution and slowed her down. For the next race she knew she had to seize her own attention, hold it in the moment to stop it from drifting ahead or behind her. She decided to say her cues out loud to herself during her warm-up runs and at the start, "otherwise I will not actually think about them." This adjustment allowed her to snap into focus and mentally connect to her three cues right from the first gate.

To clarify, our racer did not repeat her three cues at every gate, but connected, corrected, or adjusted as she bombed down the hill. She kept talking to herself about what she had to *do*. For her next race she kept her same plan, adding a little more daydreaming during the week to see herself click into her cues from gate to gate. She rated herself a 7.5 out of 10. This of course emboldened her to continue building her plan, working to stick to it, and then checking in on how she did. It became a mental talent.

You can use your plan in training too. Just as we train before an event, practice your mental approach to performance in a less competitive or pressurized environment. You won't be able to fully simulate the excitement or the stresses of the big moments, but you can improve these skills and familiarize yourself with those moments. You don't have to maintain a laser focus for an entire practice session, just for a particular drill, or the shot that isn't so easy for you. Maybe you need to plan and practice your best interviewing approach or a more direct sales pitch or be able to sit down and write the difficult part of the report you are responsible for.

Even when your event doesn't seem like a big deal, or everything seems to be going well, plan one thing to stick to. It may prevent you from later wondering what happened. Wimbledon Robyn would agree.

If you write your performance evaluations down, they are easier to track over time. But even if you only do it in your head, be sure to extract the cue or strategy you want to replicate or attempt the next time.

Ask others for their feedback if appropriate, but start to rely on evaluating yourself. If your coach, manager, parent, or colleague rates your performance significantly different from your own rating, have the discussion as to why so you can use their feedback to better gauge your performance level. They may help you by sparking an idea or confirming what needs work, but if you're courageously honest with yourself, you'll know what to work on. Get good at evaluating yourself.

Our five performers have now finished the process. We have seen them isolate their super derailers and create a master plan of skills and strategies to use under pressure. Each has planned customized focus points, but all learned to monitor their tension and use breathing at some point before and/or during their event. Remember, above all, breathing is the one skill to get good at! Here are their specific plans.

Riley's game plan

To earn more ice time Riley needed to get results. He started to use his plan in practice too. If he learned to stay present and compete well in practice, he knew he could replicate his play on game days. He would feel more satisfied and was sure his coach would notice his consistency.

Warm-up

* Do my slow it down breathing: check my tension (looking for 5 or less out of 10). If too high, do it again. If I feel too

relaxed or passive, warm up harder with ten more minutes on the bike.
* Review my facts list.
* Review my cues and *see* me doing them.
* I'm great when I keep moving my feet.
* If I make a mistake, stick to the plan.

During Game

* Move my feet.
* Finish him (initiate physical contact, finish my checks by bumping him).
* Between shifts: breathe, go over my reminders, talk to teammates to stay engaged.

#1 Focus

* Keep skating. Move my feet!

Riley's plan reflected how important his mental preparation was to a strong start. His #1 focus set the tone for his game. If he kept moving with purpose for the whole shift (to open ice, into position, chasing down the puck or a player), he would be doing his job and playing well.

Cameron's communication plan

Cameron was an accomplished teacher. She wanted to improve her ability to engage with people in new and unfamiliar settings to strengthen her confidence and her career.

Warm-up

* Body Melt breathing.
* Go over my facts list.
* See myself standing tall, arms by sides, composed.

During Event

* Introduce myself with a smile, ask questions.
* Visit more tables, network.

#1 Focus

* Listen carefully.

Cameron knew if she was listening well, she would be engaged and not overly stressing. The calmer she was, the more aware she'd be of when to move on.

Ty's conflict plan

Ty's aim was to keep himself and his coach on task. He knew this would result in a healthy exchange rather than unproductive confrontation.

Warm-up

* Check my tension, breathe it out.
* See myself sitting back in the meeting, fully explaining my position and my thoughts.
* I know we will play better if coach hears me out—make it happen.

During Meeting

* Say what I think, my ideas.
* Push back if I disagree, stand my ground.

#1 Focus

* Keep it calm!

For Ty, taking charge of his ideas was key. To do this he had to push back in a calm manner, until he was satisfied with the solutions.

Alex's game plan

When things weren't going her way, it was time for Alex to fight harder. Rather than retreat into self-sabotage and holding back, she was determined to settle into the moment and play her game, right to the finish.

Warm-up

* Pull my tension down, breathe.
* Eat!
* Daydream more! *See* my cues, don't just go through the motions, pay attention to correct technique.
* Picture myself on the specific court I will be playing on.
* Joke around with my teammates and coach to stay loose and enjoy myself.
* Remind myself to stay on my game, not look to the stands for help.

During Match

* Go to the ball! Step in and take the ball early!
* Accelerate through the shot!
* After two mistakes: go to towel box, readjust posture (no slumping!), breathe it out.

#1 Focus

* Move my feet!

Alex knew if she kept telling herself to move, to get to the ball, the rest would come naturally. To get her head ready to start the match hard, she put time into her warm-up to make sure she was ready to focus on her game.

Jamie's freak-out plan

Jamie was ready to change his reactions under pressure. The one thing he had to grab on to in the moment, to make room for a constructive response, was simply to be quiet.

Warm-up

* 4-7-8 breathing for sure.
* Stand down, Jamie, actually hear what they are saying, you do a good job when you just shut up for five seconds.
* Let it pass, don't be a jerk, be a good man.

During Meeting/Interaction/In the Moment

*   Breathe.
*   Just listen.
*   Loose face, relaxed body, good posture.

#1 Focus

*   STOP TALKING and breathe.

Jamie had to breathe and loosen, just for a moment, so he could reconnect to himself and stop talking. Every time he did this, he performed well. He was on his way.

———

With their go-to plans in place, our performers are ready for their next big event. Remember, some of these plans may work brilliantly and some may need refining. It's crucial that you check in on yourself and evaluate each performance. Be honest (really honest) about what worked, what didn't, and why. Whether a plan works as expected or not, keep going. Sometimes the plan is good, you just didn't stick to it. You can always make adjustments. And remember, when things are going well, don't mess with the plan. They went well for a reason.

Conclusion

Use Your Head

If you really want to understand being under pressure, try living and working on a nuclear submarine armed with ballistic missiles.

A young officer took a break in his Ivy League semester to join other midshipmen on a training mission deep under the sea. He told me about the uncertainty he encountered. He barely saw the sun (twice, for twenty minutes, and was glad for the vitamin D supplements he packed). He had no access to any kind of news and no outside contact with family or friends. He couldn't even find out if his dog was happy.

On the ship, there was no alone time or privacy. Options for relaxation were incredibly limited and there was a lot of time to indulge in overthinking. He didn't know when the mission would end—it could be a week, or three, or more. He would find out only twenty-four hours in advance.

In this very new and unfamiliar environment, he felt high pressure to be useful and contribute even though the trainees were mostly expected to observe, absorb, and keep themselves busy. He did not want to disrupt the crew or be that guy who made mistakes or couldn't integrate smoothly into the controlled procedures. At first his tendency was to hang back and be complacent. If he did the minimum, he could stay out of the way and avoid derailing anything. After all, the submarine would function just fine without him.

But then he thought smarter. "Why am I here?" he asked himself. He wanted his performance to be defined by what he got out of the mission and himself. He could go hide in a corner (not many of those) or participate fully. It was a challenging task, but he decided to push himself to take advantage of any opportunity.

To get the most out of this highly rich and unique experience he had to be more assertive and take initiative. He spent more time in the command center to get to know the crew. He joined the battle stations missile drills and any other exercises his superiors would allow. He asked questions. From the sonar technicians he learned how sound data could distinguish a whale from an enemy. He even sat for hours practicing steering the submarine. Not many people get to drive a submarine around the ocean.

Once back in his bunk he would reflect on his shift and evaluate his performance. His mindfulness was directed at preparing to make the most of his time on board, however long it would be. He used breathing to settle any tension he felt building in his chest as a result of a good but demanding day. He turned to happy memories and personal photos to manage any insecurities or irritability that may have surfaced. He talked to his roommates to limit the space for his mind to take a negative wander. He daydreamed. Chill and skill imagery sharpened his mindset for the next day, and he added step-it-up imagery to project himself into the high-ranking role he knew he would one day enjoy. This guy was on it!

His next training gig was nuclear power school (yes, this is a thing) to learn how to operate and manage a nuclear reactor. A little daunting and a bit of a learning curve but he would be ready to get the most out of himself because he worked to manage his mind when he felt pressure. And if he could do it in a submarine, he could do it anywhere.

The skills he used were simple and effective, and they worked best because he prepared in advance. He knew what to do when things got tough, and how to stay focused on those few actions that would get him the best results. If these skills work in the most extreme environments like this, they'll work for you, too.

He and I met only after he got back—he wanted to debrief and figure out if he could do even better in the future. I was so impressed with how much he'd figured out, and accomplished, on his own already. Once you understand this stuff, and can apply it yourself, you don't need a performance coach there beside you.

Talent does not ensure success. Nor does talent derail your performance, but a distracted mind does. In moments of stress or pressure, your skill set, technical abilities, and knowledge base don't suddenly disappear. Your talent doesn't change from day-to-day, it is your mental approach that can clutter your efforts in a relationship, an interview, the office, or on the field.

We all face pressure. And we all perform. Performing under the pressure you *feel* is the hard part. A surgeon may hold a beating heart in her hands while working to save a life, but she knows what to do. She has the training, experience, and protocols to guide her through that situation. If she feels too much stress, it is her mental approach that will allow her to do her best work and get the best results possible in that moment.

Feeling the pressure of results is unavoidable whether you are trying to organize a boisterous group of kindergarteners, standing in front of an expectant audience, or writing a book. Performing well is about making your emotions work for you, not against you. So be equipped to manage your mind! Know how to shift when you inevitably drift.

Trying to be good at any meaningful task takes courage and a focused mind. So resist the tired calls to "work harder" and use your head to work better. Determine what your *spectacular* looks like and go get it. Coach yourself, rely on yourself, motivate yourself. Know that the biggest secret to performance is that confidence is overrated. Know that the most important skill for performing with excellence is to breathe and find calm, even just a little.

Dial in, because performing well, getting results, and feeling satisfaction is a great way to nourish your mental health. And who doesn't want that?

Fun Homework

In this final section, you'll find tools to help you recognize and add to your own natural performance style. First, there are a series of questions to help you better understand yourself: where you thrive, what perhaps holds you back, and maybe hot spots you've never faced. It's all about challenging your assumptions and getting to the facts of what you *do* when things are going well, and what you need to shift away from when things aren't going so well. Take some time with these questions and be real with yourself (only you have to know).

With those truths in hand, you can start making your own performance plan, using the three-step process from part two. For a particular performance you're preparing for, you'll identify your hot spots, select the best strategies for you, and create a go-to plan you can rely on to keep you focused on the right things in the moment.

You can revisit this section as many times as you need. Your plan may only need a tweak, or it may need to be custom-made for a completely new or different performance. Try different ideas and dial in on what works best for you. Everyone is different, but these tools can and will work for anyone. Just stick to the plan!

Know Your Style

When I first start to work with clients, I often ask them some of these questions, to understand how they are built. It's important to identify what kind of performer we are so we can better get to the source of what may be getting in the way of giving our best performance.

Once you have answers, you can always refer to part one to better understand what they may say about you, and how best to use that information to your advantage. There are no wrong answers, only sincere ones.

What kind of performer are you? For these questions, rate yourself on a scale of 1 to 10 between the two ends of the continuum. No one is always all one or the other, but try to pick where you fit best. For instance, for the third question, about being either impatient or patient, an overly restless person may rate a 2 or 3 out of 10. The exact number doesn't matter as much as what it tells us about which way we tend to lean. What place on the scale better describes you? These questions will help narrow your focus to the difference makers that will help you the most. You can write your ideas in a separate notebook. But keep in mind your results may change over time and it's useful to revisit these questions to check in with yourself.

Not so good under pressure	1	....	10	Really good under pressure
Meticulous planner	1	....	10	Prefers to wing it
Impatient/Restless	1	....	10	Patient/Methodical
Impulsive	1	....	10	Disciplined
Prone to frustration	1	....	10	Stays cool
Defensive	1	....	10	Takes criticism well
Tense	1	....	10	Relaxed
Passive	1	....	10	Forceful
Quiet	1	....	10	Super chatty
Calm	1	....	10	Jumpy
Cautious	1	....	10	Risk-taker
Controlling	1	....	10	Hands-off
Avoids conflict	1	....	10	Direct/Straightforward
Will jump in and try	1	....	10	Waits for direction

With these scales in mind, try writing a brief description of yourself and your natural performance style (see chapter 1 for examples). It will help guide you as you develop your performance plan.

Fear

Fear doesn't always look dramatic or feel like panic. A person may be good at hiding it, or not even know they're afraid. Fear can manifest in different ways and it's important to understand if your performance is being affected by it. Ask yourself:

1. Are doubts or tension making me feel threatened and defensive? This could be a sign that a fear, new or old, has ratcheted up whatever stress may be normal for the situation.

2. Am I making excuses because something didn't go as well as hoped? This version of self-sabotage can become a comfortable habit. Excuses soften the reasons for failure and keep you in a state of never giving it your all. Fear of failure can cause the very failure you want to avoid.

3. Do I ignore my fears or insist I don't have any? Do you use this as a strategy to perform better? I understand the concept, but find the resolve to face your fears! Accepting them and having a plan to minimize them will enhance your performance. It may even lead to eliminating them altogether.

4. Do I try to be perfect? This is a script for failure as it simply isn't possible. Aim for excellence instead. Will you be

afraid along the way? Of course, which is just fine! Know that if you are striving in your career or relationships or in your other pursuits, at some point you will fear mistakes or failing. It is time to forget perfect!

5. What activities do I do and what interactions do I face that others would be fearful to try? Fears are relative. The things you do on a regular basis, for work or play, may be daunting to others, but more comfortable for you because you have the skills and experience to navigate the task well.

Confidence

Confidence is overrated but that doesn't mean it isn't worth paying attention to. You may have natural tendencies that can crush your confidence, so be aware of them. When you do feel your confidence slipping, ask yourself:

1. Do I feel I must find my confidence before I can perform? The reverse is true: you will find your confidence in your actions, not your feelings! The formula is: Calm + Do = Results, which leads to feeling good (a.k.a. confidence).

2. Am I making excuses? Self-deception is a way to avoid facing feelings about confidence, but you have to face reality if you're going to shift your focus from how you feel onto what you need to do.

3. Do I worry about things that haven't happened, and likely won't happen? Preparing for the worst is one thing but

dwelling on these fabricated worries distracts you from what you know will help you perform at your best level.

4. And speaking of preparation, it is possible to overprepare. Am I someone who can't leave well enough alone? A tinkerer will keep revisiting a plan, wasting time and effort that could have gone into purposeful actions. Some constantly tinker as a way to avoid getting down to actually finishing a task. If they have another option to try, they can avoid putting themselves to the test.

5. We all have self-doubts sometimes, but when under pressure do you find yourself thinking, "It won't happen for me," or, "I want this, but I probably don't deserve it"? Instead ask, "Why not me?" This mental shift can stop this self-protection in its tracks and get you back focusing on the things that matter most.

6. Do I appear confident (or at least not slumpy)? It may seem like a "fake it till you make it" argument, but adjusting your posture, breathing, and even your facial expressions can have dramatic effects on your confidence and how others around you react. It's a constructive and positive cycle that makes you and others feel better and, most importantly, ready to take action that will lead to success.

With any confidence crusher, the trick is to stop the downward drift and shift your focus from how you feel onto what you do. You can't wait for your confidence to find you. You have to go get it!

Motivation

Like confidence, motivation is something you need to do for yourself. Being motivated doesn't mean getting results. For results, you need to push past being motivated or not to actions. Ask yourself: Is my motivation only about what I *want*, or am I focused on *how* to make it happen? You need to get to the *how*. You may be highly motivated: "I want to win this vocal competition." But motivation isn't reliable on its own. Instead, focus on *how* you're going to win: "I'm going to relax my upper body, breathe low into my abdomen, and keep my neck aligned with my body so I can deliver my powerful sound—that is what I am looking for."

But what if you're not motivated? It can mean one of two things: either motivation (or a lack of it) has become an excuse for not doing your best, or you truly don't want to do something. A lack of motivation is telling you something, so find out what it is. Ask yourself:

1. Do I think strong motivation should automatically translate into good results? Is motivation a hot spot for me, as in does the pressure I feel to be good make me cling to motivation as an acceptable reason for poor results? This looks like, "No one can blame me for being lousy if I go on about how motivated and driven I am." Do I need to buckle down and focus on executing properly in the moment? Yes. Don't let motivation become a lame excuse for holding back. If you are scared, that's okay. But if you want the results that you know you can get, get around your motivation.

2. Have I lost my motivation? Or am I afraid of failure—of letting myself or others down? All performances come with a risk of failure. It's easy to convince yourself you've lost your motivation when you really haven't. The solution? Shift from how you feel to what you do!

3.   Do I really want to do this anymore? Think about what your lack of motivation is truly telling you. It's okay to quit something if the motivation really isn't there—that can be the healthy choice. Just make sure you know the real reason why before you quit.

Habits and routines

It's important to know the difference between helpful habits and routines and unhelpful superstitions. To identify if your performance behaviors are moving you forward or potentially holding you back, ask yourself:

1.   Is this action based on reason or knowledge, or is it random? If the latter, it could be anxiety driven, and it would be more productive to find an effective way to deal with that anxiety.

2.   Does this particular behavior rely on something outside my control? It's easy to blame a poor performance on something you can't control, but that never helped anyone perform better. So focus on what you *can* do and create good routines around that.

3.   Am I having trouble letting go of a superstition? If so, this could point you toward an anxiety or tension you feel when facing the unknown. That's okay! But focusing on executing actions will actually help you perform well and put the responsibility for the outcome where it belongs: in your hands.

4.   Do I have a good routine or a bad superstition? The difference is a measurable outcome. Consistent sleep

habits and general routines ensure you're rested before a big performance—that's good. But turning the light off at exactly 10:00 p.m. (not a minute earlier or later) makes no meaningful difference. Get rid of those superstitions.

Communicating

What kind of communicator are you? When trying to help someone perform better, are you giving them the help they really need? Whether it's spirited in-their-face encouragement or serious feedback, you have to communicate with care. Ask yourself:

1. Am I giving vague advice (that sounds good) or specific direction? It's the difference between "Trust yourself" and "Remember your performance cues, stick to them, you know they work."

2. Do I tend to react poorly to criticism or get defensive? Defensiveness is the most common communication issue and causes bad feelings and mistrust. Slow down and really listen, ask for clarification, and stay on topic. Solutions come from open, straightforward conversation. No matter your age, it is the responsibility of both parties to be reasonable and kind.

3. Do I raise my voice in an effort to stop a conversation? Do I yell at others when I am frustrated? Do I use sarcasm to sting or silence? If you want to connect to others (and who doesn't), control your voice and your outbursts. Take care of your own emotional backyard; you will be surprised at how well others will respond to you!

4. Am I good at calling out mistakes and errors (my own or someone else's) but forget to mention what went well? When others
are good, tell them. They will appreciate the acknowledgment.
At the same time, when you do well, enjoy it. And learn to take
a compliment with poise. All you have to say is thank you!

When you are in charge

Lessons for parents apply to everyone in a position of authority, from
mentors to managers. We all want to see our charges succeed, but despite
best intentions, hurting more than helping is a commonplace problem.
How can we avoid that? Ask yourself:

1. How much is too much? At some point, people need to be able
to execute on their own. If you've guided someone well, then
let them try to do the right thing (and get out of the way).

2. Am I causing conflict? Consider if you are overstepping or
trying to control. Think about this seriously, as a position
of power can make it easy for some individuals to flex on
others simply because they can.

3. Am I nudging or shoving? Sometimes people need a little
push, but there's a difference between helping someone be
accountable (that's good) and pushing a person too far (for
your own reasons or needs), ruining enjoyment, motivation,
or self-regard. That's obviously not good.

4. What are my motivations for this person's performance?
Am I doing this with their best interests in mind, or is

there a self-serving aspect I'm not admitting? Am I trying
to live my dreams vicariously? Do I need this person to
succeed so I can feel superior? People may not realize
they're doing this because they also genuinely care. It's
important to check in with yourself, especially if your
performer is struggling.

Red flags

When it comes to assessing others, some red flags are too big to ignore.
Maybe that person can change down the road, but it's not your responsibility to change a person, and you shouldn't have to. In the long run, what
matters as much as or even more than talent, skill, or experience is character: the ability to be self-disciplined, thoughtful, and composed under
pressure. When trying to make a responsible decision about someone else,
ask yourself:

1. Have I done my due diligence in checking references? Some
    bad reputations are warranted, and others are not, so make
    sure you've done your homework.

2. If there is an identified bad behavior, has it been repeated?
    Is there a history of bad behavior? A onetime mistake may
    be excused but repeat problems don't go away spontaneously
    (or maybe ever).

3. What can be done about a red flag in my organization?
    If avoidance isn't an option, then mitigation is important.
    Devise a plan to explain expectations, ensure accountability,
    and, if necessary, remove the individual if they can't do
    better.

Your Performance Plan

First, think about the particular performance you are planning for. Recognize when you need to shift your thinking. Our minds drift, easily and quickly, often without us being consciously aware. Combat your drift by knowing your hot spots and your super derailers: those things that sneak up on you in the moment. Once we've identified them, we can plan for them.

With clients, I offer a checklist of distractions to help them get the ideas rolling and get specific. This also shows people they are not alone. These are some of the most common, but don't stop here! Think about your performances and add your own.

STEP 1:
Identify Your Hot Spots and Super Derailers

Some common hot spots include:

- Thinking about results
- Self-doubts
- Fears (of failure, embarrassment, etc.)
- Fixating on mistakes
- Being self-critical
- Rushing
- Tension, nervousness
- Negative thoughts
- Not feeling confident
- Frustration or anger
- Worrying about what others will think
- Thinking too much
- Holding back
- Looking for excuses
- Expectations, mine and others'
- Poor preparation
- Feeling sorry for myself
- When I realize I am doing well
- Parent reactions
- Being defensive or avoidant

Add more if you need to and pick out your super derailers (your top three). Plan for those as they invade your space and hurt your performance the most. You will only need one well-thought-out plan that you can adjust as you go.

STEP 2:
Skill 1: Breathe It Out

Breathing is the most powerful and effective performance skill you'll learn. It's also the simplest. Breathing it out will ease tension in your body and mind, in seconds. You can practice breathing techniques before an event, in the days, hours, and minutes leading up to it. You can use effective breathing during performances, to control your movements, your voice, or your nerves. And after an event, good breathing can help you recover, both physically and emotionally.

There are many breathing techniques and guided exercises online and in various apps and books. Try some and use those that feel right to you. Remember to deepen your breathing by exhaling fully, exhale more air and let the inhale happen on its own. Slow it down and loosen your shoulders—get them out of your ears.

One of my favorites is slow, smooth breathing using a 4-2-4 pattern. Start by exhaling fully, blowing all the air out of your lungs. Then take a slow, easy breath, in through your nose, for a count of four seconds, then hold for two, then out through your nose for four. Repeat five or six times, more if you want. This exercise is great to do in preparation for a performance, and even in the middle of one, if it allows (e.g., fifteen-minute breaks in daylong conferences, or between pieces at your recital).

Skill 2: Performance Cues

Performance cues help us shift from how we feel to what to do. These cues are specific to the task, and different for everyone. A squash player may tell herself to keep her "shoulders down" because over a long match her tension ramps up, which affects her shot. This cue, more than any other, helps her avoid that problem.

To find your cues, take a moment to review your good performances. Think about what you did (the movements and actions or technical elements) that allowed you to excel. Drill down to the actions or behaviors that allow you to execute well. Those are the most important cues to make sure you replicate.

As you refine your skills, adjust your cues to target other elements of the performance that you want to improve. Fix one issue and then move on to the next challenge. What cues will help you in your next performance?

Skill 3: Self-Talk

Often when we think about self-talk, we think about platitudes: "You're the best" or "Everything will be fine." Those may be true, but how do they actually help? Good self-talk is task-specific.

Start with the facts, your facts. A facts list is especially useful if you're feeling doubts, because looking back on your accomplishments isn't just positive thinking, it's reminding you of useful things about yourself that are true. Facts lists can include any evidence or data about you. Results, statistics, good performances, awards, positive feedback from others, improved grades—anything that is true and pleases you to note about yourself.

When people have terrible self-talk, when they are stubbornly negative and resistant to compliments, it can be a challenge to get started on their facts. But just a little prodding can be enough to get them going. Make your list now and remember to look at it often!

The other half of self-talk is smart talk. It reminds you of your cues and stops harmful thoughts from taking hold. It doesn't have to be positive, but it must be clear: "I can do this" works, but so does "I'm going to lose if I don't calm down now, so stop holding your breath and breathe." Talk yourself through your performance. Tell yourself what to do, when to do it, and what to be ready for.

Skill 4: Daydreaming

Daydreaming isn't about staring at fluffy clouds (though that can be fun)—it's an indispensable skill for refining your talent. Think of it as mental practice. Using your imagination this way is best when it's brief, frequent, and targets specific actions. I like to talk about five imagery categories. Write down your performance-specific imagery every time you have an upcoming event:

Chill: Practicing calm (imagining a quiet room, a beach, anywhere you feel or think you would feel relaxed).

Skill: Trying a new technique, element, or rehearsing a task (imagining that excellent shot to the top corner or walking around a new venue to familiarize yourself with the environment).

Highlight: Reliving past accomplishments (remembering the details of that excellent shot or great speech or solid presentation).

Fight-back: Handling a problem (recovering from a mistake or answering a tough question).

Step-it-up: Be bold, go big (winning the game on a buzzer-beating shot or receiving that huge promotion)!

You don't have to use all of them but try different kinds of daydreaming to see what you like the most. You can do this as much as you want, and it can't hurt you! So enjoy what you create.

STEP 3:
Your Go-To Plan

It's now time to refine your lists above to create your go-to plan that you can rely on in the moment. Remember, your plan has to be short and structured. All your points in the steps above are important, but only a handful are key—that is, select those few things you know will make the difference. Your go-to plan has three sections:

Warm-up

*   A breathing exercise, and maybe something else to reduce
    tension (e.g., daydreaming).
*   Do a quick run-through of my facts list.
*   Review my cues and *see* myself doing them.
*   Some smart talk.

During Performance

*   A couple of my key performance cues.
*   If my performance allows for breaks, use them to connect
    back to anything already on my plan to keep tension down and
    sharpen focus (breathing, cues, daydreaming, etc.).

#1 Focus

*   I know that when I do this one thing, I'll execute my best.

Your plan should fit on a scrap of paper. Whether it lives in your bag,
your briefcase, your phone, or your head, refer to it often.

Post-performance, rate yourself on a scale of 1 to 10. How did you do?
Then adjust your plan for the next time as needed. If you're not sure how,
ask yourself three questions:

1. What did I do well?
2. What didn't go so well?
3. Any adjustments for next time?

Top Tips

Doing your best when it matters most is easier when you do any (or all) of the following:

* Breathe and keep breathing! Get calm and stay there.
* Forget perfection, go for excellence (or even good enough).
* It's not about how you *feel*, it's about what you *do*!
* Love your facts—keep connected to your good stuff.
* Talk your way through it.
* Keep daydreaming—see it, practice it, make it up and go big!
* Shift when you drift!
* Check in and rate your performance. Ask yourself what went well, what didn't, and note any adjustments.
* Don't chance it. Be ready for your next performance—have a go-to plan and stick to it!
* Calm + do = results!

Acknowledgments

My thanks to Kevin Hanson, President and Publisher of Simon & Schuster Canada. I am grateful for the opportunity you gave me to "go write something." I always enjoy our chats, your big ideas, and experienced counsel. Many thanks to Senior Editor Justin Stoller. I have discovered that having an editor is magnificent, especially one with excellent insight. Your ideas have made this book better. To my literary agent, Jim Levine, thank you for setting me up to get this done. I appreciate your gentle and valuable guidance.

Thank you to my wonderful parents, Myfanwy and Dr. Gary Sinclair, who have always backed me up and let me be me. What a gracious gift. To my fabulous sister, Robyn Sinclair, thank you for making use of the strategies in this book in your own competitive life and for being an overall blast to be with. Big thanks to my favorite women, Hunter Sinclair Sleeth and Morgan Sinclair Sleeth, for our entertaining discussions of your own performance stories and your very helpful comments.

My heartfelt thanks to James Sleeth this time as my spectacular and forever business partner, for reading my drafts, offering unfailingly thoughtful notes, and having a laugh as we talked through my ideas. More to come.

Finally, thank you to my clients for sharing your performance lives with me. Keep doing your thing! I always love watching you make it happen for yourselves. Because of your contributions in this book, others will see themselves in your experiences and learn that all of us can perform better and get results.

Index

About the Author

DR. DANA SINCLAIR is a founder and partner of Human Performance International, a Toronto-based management consulting firm. She's been working with athletes in pro hockey, baseball, basketball, football, and soccer since 2000, as well as high-level medical and corporate organizations. She is a licensed psychologist and holds doctorates from the University of Cambridge and the University of Ottawa. She is a clinical assistant professor with the Faculty of Medicine at the University of British Columbia and is a member of the American Psychological Association.